SOLIDARITY AND C

European Social Law in Crisis

The ongoing austerity crisis is being felt in all sectors of EU law, but has had a particularly severe impact on labour law. Silvana Sciarra, a leading judge and scholar of EU employment law, considers how solidarity regimes have been shaken by the crisis. She brings together existing European policies in social and employment law, to enhance synergies and developments in a post-crisis discourse. She looks at reactions of national constitutional courts to austerity measures and of international organizations in re-establishing respect of fundamental workers' rights. Criticizing soft law approaches in employment policies, she favours recourse to binding measures connected with selective financial incentives through European funds. She highlights developments in European sector social dialogue and new horizons of transnational collective bargaining in large multinationals. Taking a positive, practical approach, Sciarra shows how social policies can enhance solidarity and social cohesion, through European financial support.

SILVANA SCIARRA is a Judge at the Constitutional Court of Italy and was previously a Full Professor of Labour Law and European Social Law at the University of Florence and at the European University Institute. She is co-editor, with Rochelle le Roux and Bob Hepple, of *Laws against Strikes: The South African Experience in an International and Comparative Perspective* (2015).

SOLIDARITY AND CONFLICT

European Social Law in Crisis

SILVANA SCIARRA
University of Florence

CAMBRIDGE
UNIVERSITY PRESS

CAMBRIDGE
UNIVERSITY PRESS

University Printing House, Cambridge CB2 8BS, United Kingdom

One Liberty Plaza, 20th Floor, New York, NY 10006, USA

477 Williamstown Road, Port Melbourne, VIC 3207, Australia

314-321, 3rd Floor, Plot 3, Splendor Forum, Jasola District Centre, New Delhi - 110025, India

79 Anson Road, #06-04/06, Singapore 079906

Cambridge University Press is part of the University of Cambridge.

It furthers the University's mission by disseminating knowledge in the pursuit of education, learning and research at the highest international levels of excellence.

www.cambridge.org
Information on this title: www.cambridge.org/9781107450530
DOI: 10.1017/9781316091104

First published in 2013 as *L'Europa e il lavoro. Solidarietá e conflitto in tempo di crisi*, Bari-Roma, Laterza.
First published in English in 2018
First paperback edition 2019

A catalogue record for this publication is available from the British Library

ISBN 978-1-107-08606-7 Hardback
ISBN 978-1-107-45053-0 Paperback

To A. and V.
My ‘twinkling stars’

CONTENTS

PREFACE

The book I published in Italian (*L'Europa e il lavoro. Solidarietà e conflitto in tempo di crisi*, Bari–Roma, Laterza 2013) addresses issues which are still of dramatic relevance in the current discussion on austerity measures within the European Union, adopted during an unprecedented economic and financial crisis. Different discourses have been taking shape in European social law, starting from the institutional changes brought about by the Lisbon Treaty, moving to developments in the social dialogue, as well as in the implementation of employment policies. Social measures have also been at the core of emergency legislation adopted at national level.

As a consequence of all this, both the notion and the practice of solidarity have progressively changed. On the one hand, consolidated collective interests are represented by large and well-established organisations; on the other hand the aspirations of poor and socially excluded groups request to be addressed.

Contradictions, which have long been present in the European Union, are now exacerbated by the flow of immigrants and asylum seekers, escaping from wars and shortages of essential means for surviving. This is yet another difficult challenge for solidarity, which calls into question, in the first place, Member States' responsibilities.

Recourse to traditional forms of social conflict does not, by itself, unravel all such challenges, neither does it provide solutions. Therefore, solidarity and conflict carry with them new implications.

It is harder now, under such complex circumstances, to pull the red thread that keeps together my arguments, in search for alternatives, whenever the risk arises of marginalising social measures. This should be the time to thoroughly rethink the European architecture and find ways of reconciling European citizens with supranational institutions, perceived as distant and hostile. It is not my purpose to offer such a broad perspective. Neither do I intend to address the contentious topics connected with 'Brexit' and its implications in European social policies.

My intention is to show possible synergies among existing policies and to look at ways in which solidarity and conflict face new social demands. I do this looking at developments in recent years, well aware of the fact that there is a much longer history behind such events. Bibliography is intentionally selective and agile and precedence is given to documents and policy papers.

The preparation of this book, inspired by the Italian version, has been delayed, among other reasons, by a sudden change in my professional life. In November 2014 the Italian Parliament elected me to become a judge in the Constitutional Court. This meant that I had to give up my position as a Professor of European Labour and Social Law at Florence Law School and devote my energies to a new commitment.

The time lag between the Italian and the English book increases my debt of gratitude to Cambridge University Press, and in particular to Finola O'Sullivan for trusting me in the attempt to develop an updated and slightly different version of the book. I am also indebted to two blind referees who commented on my book proposal. I have taken their suggestions into account and changed in part the original structure of the Italian version.

Dr Giovanni Gruni, PhD at Oxford, now Assistant Professor, Europa Institute at Leiden University, provided a preliminary first draft of the translation from Italian into English, which I have revised, updated and, in substantial parts, rewritten. I am grateful for his initial help. However, all responsibilities for additions, omissions and mistakes are exclusively mine. Novella Caccavo, secretary at the Constitutional Court, helped me in arranging the final text, whenever we could find some time in between the preparation and editing of court cases.

The immense pride I carry with me for my new institutional responsibilities implies great respect for the Court and for all my colleagues. Opinions expressed in this book are the result of academic research I carried on. In no way do they involve the institution, which is now my home.

Rome and Florence, August 2017
S.S.

Introduction

When employment is under threat, national identities tend to consolidate around their traditional certainties, to defend what was achieved in the past and contain it within national borders. This attitude, which is not without reasons, is in contrast to the awareness that, in a globalised economy, raising barriers does not help growth and does not favour economic development.

The International Labour Organisation (ILO) – the tripartite specialised agency of the United Nations based in Geneva, where workers, employers and national governments are represented – promoted research on the social dimension of globalisation and on the effects caused by the delocalisation of productive activities towards countries with a lower cost of labour. The intention was to address the risk of imbalances among different countries and inside each of them.[1] This study, supported by very specific examples even inside the European Union (EU), has, over the years, strengthened the aspiration towards global governance, in order to promote reconciliation among social institutions and the enhancement of growth and development.[2]

However, the economic and financial crisis harshened the asymmetries in the distribution of resources in the global order. Since their origins, the European Economic Community (EEC) and then the EU tried to correct such asymmetries, despite the fact that they were born to create a common market and to assign priority to this achievement.

[1] World Commission on the Social Dimension of Globalization, *A Fair Globalization: Creating Opportunities for All* (Geneva: ILO 2004), www.ilo.org/public/english/wcsdg/docs/report.pdf; M. Delmas-Marty, 'The social dimension of globalization and changes in law', in P. Auer, G. Besse, and D. Méda (eds.), *Offshoring and Internationalization of Employment* (Geneva: ILO-IILS 2006), 187 ff.

[2] G. Gereffi, *The New Offshoring of Jobs and Global Development* (Geneva: ILO-IILS 2006) 41 ff. A broad overview of all such issues is in A. Supiot, 'What international social justice in the twenty-first century?', *Labour Law and Social Progress, Bulletin for Comparative Labour Relations*, 92 (2016), 1 ff.

The discrepancy between economic and monetary policies, on the one hand, and social policies, on the other, has been increasingly perceived by a large number of EU citizens as a gap that cannot be easily filled. Hopes vanish when the attempts to close such a gap fail. The result is widespread scepticism among European citizens, who are anxious to see how and when solidarity regimes will be reinvented in order to become more adaptable to change and suitable for reaching the aspirations of the most deprived and marginalised.

I use the word 'solidarity' in this book in order to detect ways in which collective interests emerge and are represented by organised groups at a national and transnational level. My argument implies that solidarity has been articulated, and perhaps fragmented, as a consequence of the crisis and because of changes occurring in work organisation and in the structure of the workforce. Different regimes of solidarity come into conflict with one another when social dumping is at stake. This, too, is an element for discrepancy and disillusion.

Reasons behind a generalised disaffection of citizens towards the EU are numerous and some of them will be considered in this book. A long-lasting fear addresses the fact that supranational institutions may favour the dismantling of systems of social protection at the domestic level. It is exactly for these reasons that disaffection can result in a defence of the status quo and in protectionist attitudes towards domestic orders and the rules and certitudes that they represent. In the background of this fear we can detect a system of imprecise communication between national administrations and European institutions, which has peculiar consequences for the systems of rules regulating employment relationships.

This lack of communication contradicts one of the doctrines underpinning EU law, which is intended to promote forms of mixed administration, resembling a 'cooperative federalism'.[3] A 'principle of sincere cooperation' governs the Union and Member States, according to Article 4.3 of the Treaty on European Union (TEU). Furthermore, Member States are under the obligation to adopt all measures necessary to implement legally binding Union acts, as indicated in Article 291.1 of the Treaty on the Functioning of

[3] R. Schütze, 'From Rome to Lisbon: "Executive Federalism" in the (new) European Union', *Common Market Law Review*, 47 (2010), 1385–427; R. Schütze, *From Dual to Cooperative Federalism. The Changing Structure of European Law* (Oxford University Press 2009). See also F. Fabbrini, 'From executive federalism to executive government: current problems and future prospects in the governance of EMU', in F. Fabbrini, E. Hirsch, and H. Somsen (eds.), *What Form of Government for the European Union and the Eurozone* (Oxford: Hart Publishing 2015), 289 ff.

the European Union (TFEU). In European social and employment law most sources are in fact binding and require cooperation among national administrations, in view of reaching common objectives.

The presence of collective entities – in particular the organisations representing workers and employers – makes the picture even more complex, exactly because these organisations are the expression of consolidated domestic traditions. Collective bargaining is the most relevant of these traditions because it influences the regulation of individual contracts of employment, through the production of applicable rules and standards. This also happens – and it is the case in Italy – when the dynamic process driving collective bargaining develops autonomously, with no intervention of the law.

Social partners, similarly to governments and state administrations, can easily acquire a defensive attitude to protect their own autonomy in issuing economic and normative standards. The danger is that such equilibrium could be disrupted, if competition between strong and weak systems of collective bargaining should be favoured. In all such cases, particularly when wage competition is at stake, the phantom of social dumping appears on the horizon of the internal market. This, too, is an example of imperfect communication among national administrations.

However, the opening of domestic markets should be considered as the necessary premise to the integration and mobility of undertakings and workers and as a resource for growth and competitiveness. These assumptions are not always present in the culture and practice of collective bargaining. In the same vein, it is not obvious that national bureaucratic apparatuses should support the simplification of processes of mobility and integration.

The reality is that in European discussions mixed results have been achieved with regard to the themes concerning employment and social law. The latter have not been placed at the centre of strong strategies, supported by specific budget allocations. At the crossroad of crucial choices there is an unsolved dilemma on whether to replace or adapt the numerous regulatory resources contributing to the creation of guarantees for workers. Protective measures – be they related to stability in employment, working conditions, health and safety regulation, trade union rights and the like – display the traditional function of labour and social law in the European tradition.

If we transfer this dilemma to the EU legal order, we detect a tension about an alleged subservience of social law to the rules of market integration. Hence, the question is whether the delay in the promotion of growth and employment through incisive political choices should be seen as a consequence of too strong resistance at national level in changing labour legislation, in order to foster labour market reforms.

On the other hand, free movement of undertakings, services and labour, essential leverages for market integration, has not yet generated the right rules for growth and employment. The silence of politics, incapable of producing timely decisions in the wake of an unprecedented economic and financial crisis, can generate inertia and result in short-sighted and unconstructive attitudes of the social partners.

To the contrary, the development of synergies and the promotion of new virtuous combinations of the measures to be adopted, in order to protect workers and stimulate growth, could be the right answer. The starting point is the awareness that mobility generates, both in the European internal market and in the global market, the emergence of collective interests, despite variable and often diverging regimes of solidarity. Instruments of social protection should be modulated and adapted, in order to interpret the consequences of all such global processes of mobility. However, the immense stream of migrants, carrying with them their own tragic fears and the aspiration to survive, complicates free movement across borders. An overall coherence within the EU is still missing and actions taken in order to face recurring emergencies are needed.[4]

This book is inspired by several threads in policy-making and proposes some paths for reflection, concentrating on employment and social law in the EU.

A brief overview will be offered, with regard to the choices that legislators had to make in the wake of economic and financial emergencies. In particular, the Treaty establishing the European Stability Mechanism (ESM)[5] seeks the mobilisation of funding 'to provide stability support', which can also imply entering into 'agreements or arrangements with ESM members, financial institutions or other third parties' (Article 3). Memoranda of Understanding signed with Member States undergoing financial difficulties represent yet another critical side in the discussion on solidarity during the crisis.

[4] See, among other sources, Directive 2013/33/EU of the European Parliament and of the Council of 26 June 2013 laying down standards for the reception of applicants for international protection (recast), currently under revision.

[5] The treaty to create a European Stability Mechanism (ESM) was signed on 2 February 2012.

There is little doubt that employment should be placed at the centre of growth policies. However, measures in support of employment must be traced among broad economic policies, which often blur into measures of containment of public expenditure, aiming to restabilise the equilibrium of domestic national budgets. In addition, employment policies are weakened by the lack of cooperation among national administrations and by the scarce motivation of bureaucratic elites, intervening without an effective continuity. This picture boosts the fears of European citizens and favours disaffection for Europe.

The coordination of employment policies, the so-called 'Open Method of Coordination' (OMC) should have been a key character of European new governance techniques at the opening of this century. That attempt largely failed. The confirmation for this is in the self-criticism of European institutions, obliged to recast this and other themes in a new programme called Europe 2020.[6]

I deal with the analysis of this programme in Chapter 2, with the caveat that proposals of the Commission and of the Council related to it must be contextualised within a scenario further complicated by the crisis. One important move to be highlighted concerns the reform of the European budget in the period 2014–2020, which prioritises the allocation of budget lines to projects linked with the objectives identified in Europe 2020.

Highly relevant for this analysis are measures on social cohesion emerging from research carried out in the 2009 Barca Report.[7] The ideas prompted by it are among the most pragmatic ones, when they aim to link up the creation of employment with virtuous support provided by EU structural funds.

The European Council of 30 January 2012 expressly declared the intention of supporting growth and employment through incentives to be bound to specific policy targets.[8] The Commission has gone down this path, in order to create the instruments for new forms of collaboration between the centre and the periphery of the EU with the objective of solving the asymmetries between different local realities. Accordingly, social cohesion can be considered at the same time the instrument and the final objective of European integration.

[6] Communication from the Commission, *Europe 2020. A Strategy for Smart, Sustainable and Inclusive Growth*, Brussels, 3 March 2010 COM (2010) 2020.

[7] F. Barca, *An agenda for a reformed cohesion policy, prepared at the request of D. Hubner Commissioner for regional policy*, April 2009.

[8] Informal meeting of the European Council, 30 January 2012.

In this context it is imperative to endorse, as an alternative to the competition between different solidarity regimes and the race to the bottom of wages and normative standards, a participative environment, which should favour on the one hand transnational arrangements and, on the other, national and local agreements. This proposal, used as a common thread in the following chapters, is confronted with novel functions of conflict, in particular of the right to strike.

Whoever addresses the evolution of European social policies is aware of the indissoluble nexus linking social norms and legal norms, within a complex framework of collective relationships, characterised by a constant dialogue between large organisations representing employers and workers.

Such a nexus, however, has been shaken by the gravity of the consequences of the crisis. Even before such consequences were discernible and became dramatic in their evidence, the representation of conflict and of solidarity through collective bargaining was destabilised by some judgments delivered by the Court of Justice of the European Union (CJEU). This case law will be examined in Chapter 4, mainly with the intention to highlight reactions that these decisions caused among national legislators and within national trade unions. Such reactions are symptomatic of a generalised discomfort and, at the same time, of the urgency to adapt the rules of the game whenever conflict has direct consequences on the exercise of economic freedoms.

Looking beyond the European legal order, one can listen from a distance to the dialogue going on between the Luxembourg Court, the Strasbourg Court – competent in the enforcement of the European Convention on Human Rights and Fundamental Freedoms (ECHR) – and the Committee of Experts of the ILO. This latter body, which is not a proper court of adjudication of legal disputes, has the delicate task of monitoring the application of conventions and recommendations by the Member States of the ILO. The Committee is composed of *super partes* experts, independent from national governments, and plays the role of interpreting and adapting legal norms in the context of the major changes of our times. All this is discussed in Chapter 5.

In litigation connected to the burst of the crisis, an innovative role has also been played by the European Committee of Social Rights, which administers the Council of Europe's Social Charter (ESC). The unique provision on collective complaints, provided for in the 1996 Protocol added to the revised Charter, proved to be very popular among several national unions wishing to make their voices heard in reaction to EU measures. This option was chosen, among others, by Swedish unions, in response to legislation adopted to comply with the CJEU's ruling in *Laval*, as well as by unions in bailout countries, in order to re-establish the guarantees of fundamental rights badly hit by austerity measures.

In the light of this judicial and quasi-judicial activism, I argue that the circulation of labour standards and the contamination among supranational sources is valuable and should be further pursued. The proposal for a 'European Pillar of Social Rights', put forward by President Juncker in his speech on the State of the Union, delivered on 9 September 2015 before the European Parliament (EP), drew on international sources of the Council of Europe and of the ILO and provoked positive reactions and the impulse for better synergies.[9]

With such a diverse panorama in the background, measures determining a change in social policies have to be analysed taking into account the framework and the objectives given to the process of European integration. The crisis has made it more difficult to link the threads of social law with emergency measures adopted as a consequence of austerity and budget cuts. The intense phase that has interested Europe in the aftermath of the crisis turned into an impediment to considering growth and employment in a satisfying manner. However, this project should not be abandoned. Rather, it should be a starting point in rethinking institutional changes and enhancing reforms.

[9] See ec.europa.eu/commission/publications/state-union-2015-european-commission-president-jean-claude-juncker_en.

1

Europe in Time of Crisis

1 Fear from Europe: A False Start

Employment and social protection are at the centre of several European discussions. Sometimes these themes appear elusive, blurred by the delays in the implementation of programmes and unclear in terms of the messages to be sent to citizens. The economic and financial crisis provoked widespread uncertainty and made it even more necessary to research a common ground on which to lay effective legislative initiatives. Large organisations representing the interests of workers and employers have always been concerned with building consensus and facilitating the redistribution of resources, both in terms of legal protection and of employment opportunities.

Such a delicate involvement, however, can be difficult in a changing environment as the one originated by the crisis. This is why discussions on employment cannot be separated from a more comprehensive evaluation of the policies of reform to be addressed towards the EU at large and its internal market in particular. Such reforms are now required with greater emphasis because of the repercussions caused by austerity measures in some of the bailout countries and, more broadly, as a consequence of stronger coordination of budget rules brought about by the 'Fiscal Compact'.[1] In this Treaty the promotion of employment is put forward as one segment of overall strategies that should enhance a 'proper functioning of the euro area' and contribute to the 'sustainability of public finances' and to 'reinforcing financial stability' (Article 9).

Furthermore, the dramatic increase in the flow of migrants, escaping from poverty and wars, makes all issues related to employment, social policies and social security even more central in the public sphere. Controversies arise on how and whether to redistribute resources, while facing the expansion of people requiring access to essential welfare services.

[1] Treaty on Stability, Coordination and Governance in the Economic and Monetary Union, of 2 March 2012.

In order to understand, at least in part, the fear, sometimes an irrational one, coming from Europe and detect its links with social policies, the role of social partners cannot be ignored. Especially in the countries that were the first to join the EU, unions and employers organisations contributed to the creation of national identities. At the same time, acting as representatives of general interests, they received wide legitimation by national legal systems in which they were – and still are – deeply rooted.

This characteristic of Western democracies is relevant in understanding the role that states must continue to play in empowering private bodies and ascertaining the collective interests they pursue. States are the ones who must set the rules and establish criteria to select representative and democratic organisations.

At supranational level this projection of national identities is less consolidated and, most of all, complicated by the allegiance that social partners develop towards European institutions, without losing their inborn consistency with national institutions. Behind this tension, caused by what appears to be a dilemma of split loyalty, there is a history of slow – and yet persuasive – change brought about over the years.

With the reformist agenda pursued by Jacques Delors, enthusiastic architect of social policies in the years 1985–1995 when he was President of the European Commission, social partners conquered a space of intervention in the EU, notwithstanding the express exclusion of the 'right of association' from the competences of the Treaty (now in Article 153 paragraph 5 TFEU). His imagination triggered the activism of the European organisations representing management and labour and slowly made them co-protagonists in the law-making process (now Articles 154 and 155 TFEU).

Market integration can generate protectionist reactions in political and institutional actors and drive them towards the defence of the internal equilibrium consolidated in each national legal order.[2] The same reaction can occur among trade unions and employers' organisations, which are inclined to defend domestic systems of industrial relations, especially when competition negatively affects wages and working conditions. Hence, they may very well become the ones to claim that fear comes from Europe.

In a very critical reading of European social policies, weakened by the absence of a supranational welfare state, it has been maintained that the

[2] N. Countouris and S. Engblom, 'Civilising the European Posted Workers Directive', in M. Freedland and J. Prassl (eds.), *Viking, Laval and Beyond* (Oxford: Hart Publishing 2015), 279 ff.

'neo-voluntarist' choice made in the 1990s in the reforms of the Treaties, instead of protecting the organisations of workers and employers from legislative interferences, intentionally meant to weaken their role, for reasons linked with the competitiveness of the European market.[3]

A similar radical criticism was addressed towards European institutions accused of an isomorphic obsession that, rather than supporting the diversification and growth of interest groups, favoured their conformism. Integration would have encouraged, on the basis of this narrative, the repeal of solutions aimed at the rebuilding of collective interests around new groups, so weakening domestic organisations, rather than rebuilding them at the supranational level.[4] Social partners, instead of choosing freely and voluntarily to make their voices heard, would have been swallowed through an institutional game which was not aimed at the enhancement of differences, but rather at suppressing their original identities.

In order really to grasp this radical criticism we have to recall that the choice of trade unions and of employers' organisations to proceed 'voluntarily' on paths that are independent from the law, represents a distinctive trait of the tradition in most European countries. The evolution of voluntary collective bargaining was useful to appraise trade union autonomy, a principle that is a cornerstone of the constitutions drafted in the aftermath of the Second World War,[5] as well as a fundamental right granted by the conventions of the ILO, by other relevant United Nations (UN) sources and, more specifically, Council of Europe sources.

The analysis carried out above, dense of negative predictions, appears, therefore, founded on a prejudice or maybe a false start. Such predictions have not been confirmed by subsequent history. The representation of neo-voluntarism at European level acquired characteristics that are different from what happened after the Second World War in most European countries and, in a partially different way, in the United Kingdom. On the basis of constitutional principles or, for some countries, on the basis of diffuse customs and practices, the notion of collective autonomy

[3] W. Streeck, 'Neo-voluntarism: a new European social policy regime?', *European Law Journal*, 1 (1995), 31–59. A more comprehensive critique is in W. Streeck, *Buying Time: The Delayed Crisis of Democratic Capitalism* (New-York, London: Verso Books 2014).

[4] S. Bartolini, *Restructuring Europe: Centre Formation, System Building, and Political Structuring between the Nation State and the European Union* (Oxford University Press 2005), 293–304.

[5] S. Sciarra, 'The evolution of collective bargaining: observations on a comparison in the countries of the European Union', *Comparative Labor Law and Policy Journal*, 29 (2007), 1 ff., a survey based on results of comparative research.

consolidated. The latter is a socially accepted practice and a legally effective one, when it comes to setting wages and normative standards. Furthermore, the autonomy of social partners at the national level is now acknowledged in Article 152 TFEU, a novelty brought about by the Lisbon Treaty.

1.1 Wage Policies and Pay Cuts: Constitutional Courts in the Crisis

Collective autonomy acquired with time an extraordinary foundational value, because it allowed the identification of organised groups representing collective interests, both with regard to workers and employers. In some European countries – for example in Germany, until very recently, and still in Sweden and in Italy – one of the most important results of collective autonomy consisted in doing without legislation on minimum wage and substituting it with efficient wage policies conducted by social partners.

This phenomenon can easily be affected by changes, because of a diffused decrease in the rate of affiliation to trade unions, which inevitably weakens national systems of collective bargaining. It is a reality that for a long time, albeit for different reasons, social partners refused the intervention of the legislator with regard to wage regulation and they still show resistance to such interferences.[6]

However, it is widely acknowledged that wage policies should be put at the centre of future reforms of economic governance within the EU. Cross-country coordination in wage setting was attempted, following the adoption of the single currency, as a way of absorbing asymmetric shocks,[7] but it did not produce long-lasting results. Imbalances among Member States, a visible effect of the crisis, have reopened the discussion on common initiatives to be promoted, in order to avoid wage competition and endorse wage increases.[8]

[6] European Commission, Directorate-General of Employment, Social Affairs and Inclusion, *Labour Market and Wage Developments in Europe* 2015; European Commission Directorate-General for Employment, Social Affairs and Inclusion Unit B.1, *Industrial Relations in Europe 2014*, 41 ff.

[7] L. Calmfors, 'Wages and wage-bargaining institutions in the EMU. A survey of the issues' *Empirica*, 28 (2001), 325 ff. A complete reconstruction of these attempts is offered in, L. Bordogna and R. Pedersini, 'What kind of europeanization? How EMU is changing national industrial relations in Europe', *Giornale di diritto del lavoro e di relazioni industriali*, 146 (2015), 189 ff.

[8] 'Nominal unit labour costs have been falling in countries having to rebalance their economies after periods of large current account deficits. Cyprus, Greece, Slovenia and

With a change of direction that must be highlighted, the European Commission, aware of such negative impact of the economic crisis on wage policies, has insinuated in its country-specific recommendations to the Council[9] that minimum wage legislation should become part of national reforms, both for a potentially beneficial impact on employment and for shortening distances across different regions.

The example of Germany is paramount in combining compliance with the Commission's initiative and urgency to acknowledge domestic political instability. The Chancellor, eager to consolidate political support in a newly established large coalition, rapidly translated the Recommendation issued in 2012 into law. The law adopted in 2014 came into effect on 1 January 2015. Commentators argued for potential spillover effects on other countries, in particular with regard to low-skilled workers.[10]

The departure from a consolidated previous practice was criticised by trade unions, but came as a consequence of the decline in the number of workers covered by collective agreements. The impact of this reform, according to critics, could, in the long run, cause the loss of jobs. Hence, it should be monitored with special attention to vulnerable groups in the labour market, such as young and unskilled workers and those employed in the former East Germany, where salaries lower than in the rest of the country are paid. Furthermore, the new law provides for many exceptions – trainees, long-term unemployed, and workers under eighteen years of age – and excludes for a two year period some sectors of the economy.

However, research provided after the enforcement of the law shows that even collective bargaining benefited from minimum wage legislation, contributing to the increase of the lowest wage groups. Moreover, marginal part-time employment – the so-called mini jobs – declined.[11] This observation of the German case runs parallel to the concern shown by the European Central Bank (ECB) with regard to low wages and with the renewed interest in coordinated collective bargaining to fight price instability.[12]

Spain recorded marked declines in nominal unit labour costs in 2014, while strong increases took place in the Baltics and Slovakia'. See European Commission, *Labour Market and Wage Developments*, supra n. 6, 3.

9 See at Section 2.1, for the procedures enshrined in the European Semester, aimed at addressing recommendations to individual member states.

10 V. Pop, 'Germany adopts minimum wages', 3 July 2014, euobserver.com/economic/124865.

11 M. Amlinger, R. Bispinck, and T. Schulten, 'The German minimum wage: experiences and perspectives after one year', *WSI-Report*, 28, 1 (2016).

12 R. Janssen, 'Central banks warm to collective bargaining', 30 March 2016, www.socialeurope.eu/2016/03/43370.

It is noteworthy that, in the case of the German reform, internal politics reacted to criticism from abroad, in the attempt to enhance demand-side measures.[13] 'Fear from Europe', felt by national unions as an imposition on free collective bargaining, translated into a quick response from the legislature, which intended to create political stability.

A different implication is the one connected to the effects of austerity measures adopted during the crisis and addressed to the reduction of wages. The lack of resources and the need to reduce public spending were at the origin of wage moderation and wage cuts.

For example, in Greece the reduction of minimum wages stipulated in collective agreements, brought workers younger than twenty-five years below the poverty line. This measure was challenged by the trade unions as discriminatory on the ground of age (Article 1.2) and as contrary to the 'right to a fair remuneration' (Article 4.1 ESC).[14]

Measures adopted by the Greek government in 2012 were such to abolish collective bargaining for the definition of minimum wages, since they assigned to the government a unilateral power to reduce salaries.

The Greek Council of State, departing from its early case law, in which it ruled as constitutional a large part of austerity measures on the ground of exceptional and temporary circumstances, struck down wage cuts imposed by the Greek government in 2012 on the police and armed forces as part of the conditions for the bailout programme. The Court found that cuts imposed by the Memorandum of Understanding (MoU) exceeded the limits set by the Constitution on grounds of proportionality and equality in imposing a public burden.[15]

Comparative research shows that in bailout countries challenges on wage cuts have been brought on different constitutional basis, ranging from the right to work, the right to property, equal participation in dealing with a public burden, the right to dignity and the rule of

[13] R. Thillaye, 'In search of public approval. strengthening governance and legitimacy in the eurozone', *Policy Network Paper*, December 2014.

[14] Collective complaints 65 (2011) and 66 (2011) *(ECSR, General federation of employees of the national electric power corporation (GENOP-DEI) and Confederation of Greek Civil Servants' Trade Unions (ADEDY)* v. *Greece*) were decided on 23 May 2012. References in M. Yannakourou, 'Challenging austerity measures affecting work rights at domestic and international level. The case of Greece', in C. Kilpatrick and B. de Witte (eds.), *Social Rights in Time of Crisis in the Eurozone: The Role of Fundamental Rights' Challenges', Special Issue European Journal of Social Law*, 12 (2014), 25 ff.

[15] Decisions 2192–2196, 13 June 2014 EurWORK, European Observatory of working life, 16 October 2014, www.eurofound.europa.eu/it/observatories/eurwork.

law.[16] The implication is that austerity measures have, in different ways and to different degrees, shaken the internal equilibrium of national constitutional orders and have given ground to a creative, albeit discontinuous, constitutional case law. Wages, in particular, call into question the guarantee of freedom of association and the right to collective bargaining.

The Portuguese Constitutional Court, in twelve decisions taken in different phases of the crisis, ruled on pay cuts for public sector workers in the years from 2011 up to 2015. Cuts and other forms of economic reductions, described as solidarity measures, also affected retired people. In the latter cases the Court had to take into account legitimate expectations of the pensioners and consider this a relevant argument in ruling unconstitutional both the 2012 and the 2013 articles in the state budget laws.

As for pay cuts in the public sector, the Court's case law can, at first sight, appear incoherent. However, differences in the rulings are justified by the reiteration of the reductions imposed on public employees. Whereas in a first decision (396/2011) the Court declared constitutional limited sacrifices, rejecting the violation of the principle of equality, in a second one (353/2012) it found that additional cuts could not be justified by the urgency to pursue public interest. However, the ruling was effective for 2012 and not for the past, due also to the fact that the previous pay cuts were maintained. The Head of State, among others, challenged the state budget law for 2013 before the Court, alleging that wage cuts were in violation of the 'proportional equality' principle, since they could be assimilated to taxes. The Court rejected this claim and held the law unconstitutional on the ground of unequal treatment, since pay cuts only hit public sector workers.

It is worth mentioning that proportional equality – a new terminology adopted by the Court in the so-called case law of the crisis – clearly represents the adaptations required to legal reasoning in exceptional circumstances. Inequality caused by compliance with European obligations – the Court maintained – should be accepted as long as it is proportional.[17]

[16] C. Kilpatrick, 'Constitutions, social rights and sovereign debt crisis in Europe: a challenging new area of constitutional inquiry', EUI Working Papers, Law 34/2015, and the special issue of *European Journal of Social Law*, 12 (2014) supra n. 14, in particular the chapter by C. Kilpatrick and B. De Witte, 'A comparative framing of fundamental challenges to social crisis measures in the Eurozone', 3 ff. See also K. Tuori and K. Tuori, *The Eurozone Crisis. A Constitutional Analysis* (Cambridge University Press 2014).

[17] A. M. Guerra Martins, 'Constitutional judge, social rights and public debt crisis', *Maastricht Journal of European and Comparative Law*, 22 (2015), 695–6. The author is a former judge in the Portuguese Constitutional Court.

Finally, Parliament asked the Court to scrutinise the constitutionality of new pay cuts, which should have replaced the ones imposed in 2011 and enforced throughout 2013, addressed to low-income workers. The Court found in this case that the violation of the equality principle was even more striking; however, the ruling was effective only for the future. The immediate reaction by Parliament was to put forward a new proposal, establishing pay cuts until 2018, albeit in a gradual way. Here the Court argued that the obligation, arising from membership of the EU, to avoid excessive deficit does not diminish a state's discretion in choosing the appropriate measures and in doing so in compliance with the Constitution. Hence, pay cuts prolonged for the years 2016–2018 were no longer a temporary measure and were, because of this, to be held unconstitutional.

The apparent incoherence in this complex series of cases is, in fact, a clear sign of the attention paid by the Court to balancing public burdens with constitutional rights. While paying homage to EU law and to the MoU signed by Portugal, the Court maintains a margin of appreciation, which is significant enough to justify its own institutional mission in enforcing fundamental principles, common to constitutional traditions in other Member States. It has been noticed, however, that dissenting opinions have become more numerous; this may be the sign of an increasing uneasiness among the judges in balancing different priorities over such a long time.[18]

This difficulty is confirmed by the fact that the General Confederation of Portuguese Workers filed parallel complaints to the ILO, as a reaction to measures agreed in the MoU (section 7 Act No. 23/2012), changes introduced in the 2009 Labour Code and wage cuts in the public sector. The ILO Committee of Experts on Freedom of Association, while acknowledging the attempts made by the Portuguese government to enhance social dialogue, had to address the issue of wage cuts and recommend that the government promoted an impact evaluation of the law.[19] It is worth recalling that recourse to international sources comes as a reaction to the CJEU's refusal to answer preliminary references filed by Portuguese courts, since the latter had failed to demonstrate

[18] M. Canotilho, T. Violante, and R. Lanceiro, 'Austerity measures under judicial scrutiny: the Portuguese constitutional case-law', *European Constitutional Law Review*, 11 (2015), 183.

[19] Commentary of the decision in Case No. 3072 (Report No. 325) delivered on 13 June 2014 by D. Abrunhosa e Sousa, 'Portuguese labor austerity measures and the principle of freedom of association', *International Labor Rights Case Law*, 2 (2016), 136–41.

that measures adopted in compliance with the MoU were implementing EU law.[20]

It is interesting to point out that judicial activism took place even in countries which were not signatories of MoUs, but were under severe budgetary restrictions and had to adopt austerity measures.

The Italian Constitutional Court ruled unconstitutional a wage freeze in the public sector, implemented as a quick and efficient response to the crisis in 2011 and then prolonged in the following years. The laws which originally introduced the wage freeze and all subsequent measures were found contrary to freedom of association (Article 39 paragraph 1 of the Constitution).

In Italy public sector unions negotiate salaries with a special public body representative of state administrations. The latter must follow the government's assessment to set aside the necessary economic resources, in order to start negotiations.[21] Such resources were never set aside in budget laws subsequent to the original wage freeze, thus impeding the exercise of the right to bargain, which is strictly connected to the exercise of freedom of association.

Because of the lack of resources, due to the lack of governmental initiative, no collective bargaining had taken place following the original measure adopted in 2011. In holding unconstitutional the original law and all subsequent enforcements of the wage freeze, the Court explicitly states that its own ruling will be enforceable in the future, thus imposing an obligation on the government to act consequentially.[22] The implications of the Court's decision are closely connected to the peculiarities of collective bargaining and to the on-going, open function of negotiations, which are autonomously carried on by representatives of administrations and of workers. The choice to make the judgment only enforceable in the future – a technique which is not too common in the Italian court's tradition – shows respect for the

[20] R. Cisotta and D. Gallo, 'The impact of the Troika's austerity measures on the Portuguese labour law system: a general assessment on the scope of social sovereignty in the light of the Constitutional Tribunal case law', *European Journal of Social Law*, 1 (2014), 103.

[21] A description of the Italian public sector is provided by L. Bordogna, 'The uncertainties of endless reform: which public service employment relations after austerity?' in S. Bach and L. Bordogna (eds.), *Public Service Management and Employment Relations in Europe* (Abingdon: Routledge 2017), 84–111.

[22] An English translation of the Italian Constitutional Court's ruling 178/2015 can be found at www.cortecostituzionale.it/documenti/download/doc/recent_judgments/S178_2015_en.pdf; comments in G. Frosecchi, 'The supremacy of the right to collective bargaining: a judgment of the Italian Constitutional Court on austerity measures', *International Labor Rights Case Law*, 2 (2016), 313–18; F. Trillo Párrago, 'Políticas de austeridad y negociación colectiva en el sector público. Algunas reflexiones en torno a la experiencia Italiana', *Revista de derecho social*, 71 (2015), 201–18.

autonomy of negotiators and for budgetary policies agreed at a critical time of the crisis. At the same time, the Court confirms the centrality of a fundamental social right, notwithstanding economic constraints.

Negotiations have been reopened following the Court's ruling, and new resources have been promised, with a special emphasis on prioritising increases for low-wage workers. The follow-up to the Constitutional Court's ruling is entrusted to the negotiators, whose initiative is dependent on the government's budgetary policies. Hence, the concrete enforcement of the judgment may – as it happens – take a long time and create a vacuum of legislative initiative.

The point to underline here is that in Italy, similarly to what happened in Portugal, the stretch of time in which austerity measures should be enforced becomes a crucial point to address in constitutional adjudication. Sacrifices justified by the crisis on a temporary basis, become unreasonable when prolonged for too long, since they infringe the fundamental right to organise and bargain collectively. The Italian Constitutional Court's ruling makes express reference to significant international and EU sources, as a confirmation of the linkages that keep together labour standards and of the urgency to recall them all, when exceptional circumstances occur.

The Spanish *Tribunal Constitucional* also had to face challenges related to austerity measures, in particular reduction of public spending, non-re-evaluation of pensions and a 5 per cent reduction of public sector salaries. Decree 8/2010 was considered in breach of Article 28.1 and 37.1 of the Spanish Constitution, namely of freedom of association and the right to collective bargaining. Both provisions are included in Part I of the Constitution and should, as fundamental rights, not be addressed by Decrees. The Court ruled, however, for the constitutionality of the measures adopted, arguing for the primacy of laws, as opposed to collective agreements, in the hierarchy of sources and submitting that collective agreements are, by definition, subject to changes.[23]

In a subsequent decision,[24] prompted by a trade union's action before an administrative court, the *Tribunal Constitucional* dismissed other

[23] Tribunal Constitutional ATC 85/2011. A critical appraisal of this ruling is in M. L. Rodriguez, 'Labour rights in crisis in the Eurozone: the Spanish case', *European Journal of Social Law*, 1 (2014), 131. See the dissenting opinion expressed by Judge F. Valdés dal Ré, 'Voto particular que formula el Magistrado don Fernando Valdés Dal-Ré a la sentencia dictada en el recurso de inconstitucionalidad núm. 4123-2012', *Boletìn Oficial del Estado* (2016) 196, www.tribunalconstitucional.es.

[24] ATC 179/2011. Comments in S. Cocchi, 'Constitutional courts in the age of crisis. A look at the European Mediterranean area', *Rivista di Diritto Pubblico Italiano Comparato Europeo* (12 November 2014) 18, www.federalismi.it.

claims of unconstitutionality, grounded on the violation of the equality principle (Article 14) and on the assumption that reduction of salaries are a hidden form of taxation, limited to public sector employees only, in breach of the principle of progressive imposition of taxes (Article 31) and of the right to private property (Article 33).

This brief analysis of selected cases explains why the role played by constitutional courts can be perceived as a 'risk'.[25] The issue at stake is independence of the judiciary from political contingencies and the need to rebalance political priorities within a coherent constitutional framework. Recourse to bodies different from national judiciaries confirms that an international nexus keeps together rights and principles and constitutes a barrier against irrational and too extreme choices made by domestic legislatures, put under pressure because of the crisis.

In particular, wage cuts in the public sector and in low pensions may end up hitting an impoverished middle class and expand the number of people exposed to social exclusion. Solidarity, in this case, means to rethink the notion of security, automatically linked to salaries and pensions, and discuss the justification at the origin of austerity measures, whereby earnings based on individual and collective rights are described as privileges, if compared with worse social disadvantages.

It is useful to recall, in this regard, that pay is expressly excluded from the competences of the TFEU (Article 153 paragraph 5). Accordingly, the invitation of the Commission in country-specific recommendations, within the framework of the European Semester, has a mere exhortatory value, which should not affect the autonomy of collective actors at domestic level and certainly cannot result in a legislative initiative at European level. One could argue, in this regard, that there has been a delay of national trade unions in taking action and starting a comprehensive reflection on the urgency, in time of crisis, of boosting instruments for wage increases and for the setting of minimum wages. More equitable regimes would be established, with a view to avoiding 'poverty traps' that attract less qualified workers towards low wage levels and promote consumption.

For all these reasons, despite difficulties in collecting data on wage bargaining and in measuring reductions in wage growth in connection

[25] See again C. Kilpatrick, 'Constitutions, social rights and sovereign debt crisis in Europe', supra n. 16, and the special issue of *European Journal of Social Law*, 12 (2014), supra n. 14.

with reduced productivity,[26] wage monitoring should be part of economic governance and be interrelated to balanced fiscal policies.[27]

Social inequalities, which are due, among other reasons, to differences in wages and to difficulties in including the weakest among those who earn decent salaries, cannot be ignored. The proposals to formally insert a clause on wage standards in the reformulation of EU economic policies should contrast social dumping and stop the dangerous decline of wage levels. Sanctions should be inflicted on Member States, similarly to what is done for countries with a high public debt.[28] Wage policies, even during times of crisis, enhance solidarity and contrast poverty. Best practices throughout the EU suggest that law should be supportive of collective bargaining and instrumental to their autonomous choices.

In order to confirm that collective autonomy still represents an added value in the evolution of European social law, some recent outcomes of the social dialogue will be presented in the following section. The suggestion is that 'fear from Europe' should not stop the initiatives of social partners, neither should it diminish their influence in policy-making. These results contrast, however, with the weak role played by European organisations representing management and labour in the economic governance of the EU during the most dramatic phases of the crisis.

1.2 Achievements of European Social Partners: Sector Social Dialogue

Perspectives taken by the social partners within the framework of EU law are peculiar and original, when placed in a comparative perspective. The slow mood of Treaty amendments progressively disclosed a completely new organisation of supranational collective interests. The latter are built around a partial delegation of powers that the Treaties conferred to social partners (Articles 154 and 155 TFEU).

More value has also been added to the autonomy of collective bargaining, which can express itself on the basis of variable forms and contents, for

[26] European Commission, *Industrial Relations in Europe*, supra n. 6, 50–4.

[27] A. Watt, 'European economic governance: what reforms are to be expected and what are needed?', (2010) *European Alternatives*, www://euroalter.com.

[28] E. Brancaccio, 'For a European Wage standard', in *Foundation for European Progressive Studies, Austerity is Not the Solution. Contributions to European Economy Policy, Renaissance*, 2 (12 October 2012), 75 ff. at www.feps-europe.eu/assets/9549a450/austerity-is-not-the-solution.pdf and on file with author.

instance through the so-called European sector agreements, dealing with a great variety of subject matters, within specific areas of economic and service activities.

Since 1998 the European Commission promoted the expansion of these peculiar voluntary sources, indicating criteria of 'representativity' – it is worth recalling this neologism – and organisational formulas designed to guarantee the rooting of all sector committees in national systems of industrial relations.[29] In recent years there was an evident expansion of this practice, followed by the strengthening of sector agreements, intervening in certain areas, on specific subject matters, at European level.

For example, the social partners in air transport were successful in influencing European institutions on changes to be introduced in existing regulations,[30] in order to adopt the 'home base' criterion as the only one in determining the applicable regime of social security for flight crew and cabin crew members. This measure, which may at first sight appear a marginal one, aims, on the contrary, at coordinating social security and creating legal certainty in a very critical area of transport, in which litigation has been frequent in the last few years. It may indirectly also acquire relevance for the identification of the place where work is habitually performed and for the competent legal courts on the law applicable to contracts of employment.[31]

Moving to a different sector, a 2012 framework agreement was signed in the social dialogue committee for central government administrations. It identified twenty commitments to update Protocol No. 26 on Services of general interest, in compliance with the fundamental right to good administration and in response to budgetary constraints during the crisis.[32]

[29] Commission Decision 98/500 CE of 20 May 1998 on the establishment of Sectoral Dialogue Committees promoting the Dialogue between the social partners at European level, OJ L 225/27, 1998. Empirical research is referred to in E. Léonard, E. Perin, and P. Pochet, 'The European sectoral social dialogue: questions of representation and membership', *Industrial Relations Journal*, 42 (2011) 254 ff.

[30] Regulation (EU) No. 465/2012 of the European Parliament and of the Council of 22 May 2012 amending Regulation (EC) No. 883/2004 on the coordination of social security systems and Regulation (EC) No. 987/2009 laying down the procedure for implementing Regulation (EC) No. 883/2004, OJ L 149, 8 June 2012.

[31] Social dumping in air transport is addressed in Joined Cases C-168/16 and C-169/16, *Sandra Nogueira and Others* v. *Crewlink Ltd* and *Miguel José Moreno Osacar* v. *Ryanair*, 14 September 2017. The AG's Opinion maintains that disputes on contracts of employment for crew members are within the jurisdiction of courts where work is performed, namely where workers start and end their working days. The CJEU finds the 'home base' concept an 'indicium' for determining the workplace.

[32] The text of the agreement is accessible at www.epsu.org/sites/default/files/article/files/PR_2012_12_19_SDCCGAagreement_-EN-2.pdf.

Finally, in 2012 *Eurociett* and *Unieuropa global union* – these are the social partners in the temporary agency sector – carried on a project on labour market transitions in Europe and produced recommendations to EU policy-makers. They aimed at prompting better cooperation between private and public employment agencies, an issue recognised as a central one in reforming labour markets for boosting employment. As an outcome of sector social dialogue, these social partners were able to influence the proposal for a regulation.[33]

All such examples, which may appear random and limited in their achievements, confirm nevertheless that measures originated by sector social dialogue are not extraneous to the crisis. They tackle relevant issues, which in different ways have to do with creating employment opportunities and establishing fair working conditions. A broader implication of these practices has to do with the ability of social partners to best exploit their quasi-institutional role, namely to act as representative organisations within a legal framework, while preserving their autonomy.

In the attempt to fight against the fear coming from Europe, results achieved by the social partners are forward looking, because they confirm that collective autonomy is a resource within the EU. The autonomy of social partners operating within the framework of sector collective bargaining is a sign of institutional pluralism, at different levels. Both primary EU law (Article 152 TFEU) and secondary law, as for the previously mentioned 1998 Commission's Decision, support a consensual system in which labour standards are identified and may open the way to legislation.

Sector agreements could be further expanded and become an instrument to regulate working conditions. For instance, among the leverages identified by the Commission to boost the internal market and favour the mobility of workers, we find procedures for the recognition of professional qualifications, to be encompassed in a European framework of certifications.[34] Sector European agreements could constitute the ideal

[33] See European Commission, Social Europe, Newsletter No. 5, January 2014, 90–2. The Commission proposed a Regulation, based on Article 46 TFEU, which should facilitate labour mobility through EURES. See Proposal for a Regulation of the European Parliament and of the Council on a European network of Employment Services, workers' access to mobility services and the further integration of labour markets /* COM/2014/06 final - 2014/0002 (COD).

[34] Communication from the Commission to the European Parliament, the Council, the Economic and Social Committee and the Committee of the Regions, *Single Market Act. Twelve levers to boost growth and strengthen confidence. 'Working together to create new growth'*, Com (2011) 206 final, 13 April 2011, 7. Further references in European

place for this and other experiments of supranational standardisation, in order to facilitate the mobility of workers. It is of utmost importance that organisations involved in standard-setting agreements are representative, according to the criteria indicated by the Commission.

In the light of such evolving policies, fear coming from Europe can be, at least in part, dissolved if we acknowledge that places for the development of supranational consensus can be set up and function efficiently. This issue will come back further on, in the overview of transnational collective agreements. This new format of bargaining adds to the already existing levels of negotiations, both at national and European level.[35]

Meanwhile, it is possible to reconsider the 'false start' mentioned at the beginning of this chapter and oppose to the fear coming from Europe, by trusting in a potential expansion of collective bargaining, meant as a network of exchanges, in which the aggregation of interests takes place within and outside national borders.

These are the preconditions to building new solidarity regimes. The emergence of new levels of bargaining, originated by large organised groups representing management and labour, should not be perceived as a force destabilising national legal systems and social sub-systems that have grown and developed within states. To the contrary, this process should be proposed as a positive signal, going, as it does, in the direction of building on changes and letting collective interests emerge, with a view to establishing new regimes of transnational solidarity.

Some food for thought in this direction can be retrieved in the proposals for the adoption of the Single Market Act received, even if slowly, by the Commission.[36] The actions of reform – the twelve levers for growth – concerned, among other issues, the full compatibility, on the one hand, of the exercise of the right to bargain collectively and of the right to strike and, on the other, the protection of the fundamental economic freedoms granted by the Treaty. Premise for a reconsideration of such collective rights is the mobility of workers, free from the influences of rigid national labour markets, which have little propensity for the reception of workers

Commission, *Industrial Relations in Europe 2010* (Luxembourg: Publications Office of the European Union 2011).

[35] See Chapter 3.

[36] On 13 April 2011 the Commission adopted the Single Market Act. Communication from the Commission: 'Single Market Act: Twelve levers to boost growth and strengthen confidence: Working together to create new growth', COM(2011)206/4. A new proposal for a Single Market Act II followed in 2012. See eur-lex.europa.eu/legal-content/EN/TXT/PDF/?uri=CELEX:52012DC0573&from=EN.

or for letting them leave the country. Critics of negative developments within EU social policies are fully aware of the fact that, even before the burst of the crisis, vast uneasiness was originated by the CJEU's case law limiting the right to strike, when freedom of establishment and freedom to provide services were at stake.[37]

Controversial developments, originated by this case law, will be analysed further on.[38] One conclusion to be drawn now is that, rather than breaking down regimes of solidarities, the exercise of economic freedoms should favour the harmonisation of standards, with regard, in particular, to wages and working conditions.

In the light of the initiatives going on,[39] one can reasonably oppose the fear coming from Europe and try to reverse the false start that it may create. With this objective in mind, I have highlighted the constructive activism of the social partners, which gave rise to positive, albeit too limited, outcomes. It is worth underlying that social dialogue rests on the assumption that the actors involved in it are 'representative'. The

[37] Case C-438/05, *International Transport Workers' Federation and Finnish Seamen's Union* v. *Viking Line ABP and OÜ Viking Line Eesti* [2007] ECR I-10779, Judgment of the Court (Grand Chamber) of 11 December 2007, and Case C-341/05, *Laval un Partneri Ltd* v. *Svenska Byggnadsarbetareförbundet, Svenska Byggnadsarbetareförbundets avdelning 1, Byggettan and Svenska Elektrikerförbundet* [2007] ECR I-11767, Judgment of the Court (Grand Chamber) of 18 December 2007, followed by other two cases, Case C-346/06, *Dirk Rüffert* v. *Land Niedersachsen* [2008] ECR I-01989, Judgment of the Court (Second Chamber) of 3 April 2008, and Case C-319/06, *Commission of the European Communities* v. *Grand Duchy of Luxemburg* [2008] ECR I-04323, Judgment of the Court (First Chamber) of 19 June 2008. More recently Case C-549/13, *Bundesdruckerei GmbH* v. *Stadt Dortmund*, of 18 September 2014. Literature on the so-called 'Laval-saga', is immense and it is impossible to give full account of it. An overview is in A. Bücker and W. Warneck (eds.), *Reconciling Fundamental Social Rights and Economic Freedoms after Viking Laval Rüffert* (Baden Baden: Nomos 2011).

[38] See Chapter 4.

[39] The EU Council on 4 December 2013 reached an agreement on the Proposal for a Directive of the European Parliament and of the Council on the enforcement of Directive 96/71/EC concerning the posting of workers in the framework of the provision of services [1997] OJ L18/1, and on 5 March 2014 the Permanent Representatives Committee of the Council of the EU approved the compromise text of the Directive, provisionally agreed between the Greek Presidency of the Council and the European Parliament: Directive 2014/67/EU of the European Parliament and of the Council of 15 May 2014 on the enforcement of Directive 96/71/EC concerning the posting of workers in the framework of the provision of services and amending Regulation (EU) No. 1024/2012 on administrative cooperation through the Internal Market Information System ('the IMI Regulation'). Directive 2014/67 deals with issues such as fraud, circumvention of rules and exchange of information. Further changes have been agreed at the Council's meeting of 23 October 2017.

acknowledgement of this characteristic is central for the recognition of the social partners' bargaining power and for the standard-setting function they fulfil in bringing negotiations to a successful result.

It is now time to connect the slow evolution of European social policies with changes occurring in the institutional framework. The departure from a traditional European legal method has been caused by the crisis and by the adoption of several emergency measures. This is why there is 'fear of Europe' and a growing urgency to establish effective antidotes to the spreading of disillusion among European citizens.

2 The Fear of Europe: The Institutional Framework

All reflections on the evolution of social policies in Europe cannot disregard a reference to the important institutional reforms that happened along the way through progressive adaptations of the Treaties. Such amendments aimed, albeit in limited means, to reinforce the role of supranational collective actors – the social partners – and to extend the legal basis in the Treaties, in order to facilitate the adoption of legislation. However, the 'fear of Europe' and of the many contradictions, which have not been solved, remains present in numerous circles and has been extraordinarily boosted by the crisis and by other dramatic events prompted by an unstable international equilibrium.

In order to partially dissolve this fear and use a light touch, we can recall the metaphor of a play performed in a theatre, where the background is changed, the scenography is improved, actors are turned over and the text of the play is regularly modified. The play is at risk of losing its internal coherence, but it may gain the strength of a constantly increased inventiveness, a play in progress, a happening, which should respond to changing expectations of the audience.

This proposed imaginary representation of the EU legal system starts with the amendments included in the Lisbon Treaty, adopted on 13 December 2007 and entered into force on 1 December 2009. As we will see, the text of the play has then been modified during the long economic and financial crisis. The exercise of recapitulating all such changes aims at showing weaknesses and strengths of the current institutional set up, shaken by the uneasiness of some countries in accepting the obligations arising from membership in the EU.

Article 3 TEU refers to the objective of 'full employment and social progress and a high level of protection', as essential elements of the 'social market economy'. The Union combats 'social exclusion and discrimination', in the perspective of gender equality and generational solidarity. With the intention to pursue such objectives, the Treaty of Lisbon introduced the so-called horizontal social clauses (Articles 8 and 9 TFEU), which intend to reiterate all the EU's obligations with respect and promotion of fundamental rights. Article 9, in particular, provides an innovative technique, whereby, in the definition and in the implementation of all 'activities' and 'policies' the Union has to take into account the 'promotion of a high level of employment' and the guarantee of 'adequate social protection'. Reference is also made to the 'fight against social exclusion' and to the promotion of 'a high level of education, training and protection of human health'.

The proclamation of all such obligations, which link together respect for fundamental rights and policy objectives, does not clarify how Articles 8 and 9 TFEU can be enforced. However, they should be read in conjunction with the rights and principles included in the Charter of Fundamental Rights, which has now the same legal value of the Treaty (Article 6 TEU).

Article 6 TEU, paragraphs 2 and 3, provides for the accession of the Union to the ECHR, without modifying the competences that had already been attributed to the Union by the Treaties. Reference to this relevant international source intersects the continuous mention in European sources of the 'constitutional traditions common to Member States'. Accordingly, everything seems to imply that the Lisbon Treaty provides a more solid legal framework for rights and principles. This process could positively influence the evolution of European social law and favour a fertile circulation of international standards.[40] However, accession to the ECHR, which the EU, now entitled with legal personality, started to pursue, was somewhat arrested by the CJEU's Opinion 2/2013, delivered on 18 December 2014.[41] The metaphor of a play in progress seems, at this regard, evocative and able to capture our imagination on the possible endings of the story.

Article 151 TFEU opens the Title in the Treaty dedicated to social policy.[42] It includes among the objectives of the Union and of Member

[40] N. Bruun, K. Lörcher, and I. Schömann (eds.), *The Lisbon Treaty and Social Europe* (Oxford: Hart Publishing 2012).

[41] Opinion pursuant to Article 218 (11) TFEU – Draft International agreement – Accession of the European Convention for the Protection of Human Rights and Fundamental Freedoms – Compatibility of the draft agreement with the EU and FEU Treaties.

[42] In C-126/86, *Fernando Roberto Giménez Zaera* v. *Institut Nacional de la Seguridad Social and Tesorería General de la Seguridad Social*, Judgment of the Court (Sixth Chamber) of 29 September 1987, paragraph 14 the ECJ indicated the binding nature of this article,

States the 'promotion of employment' and of 'improved living and working conditions'. The article refers in its opening lines to the ESC. This source has acquired renewed attention during the crisis and has offered the ground for filing several collective complaints.

This unique procedure, provided for in the 1995 Protocol annexed to the Charter, allows organised groups – not individuals – to file complaints and address them to a committee of independent experts. In order to file a complaint, organisations need to be 'representative', in accordance with Article 2.1 of the Protocol and must have competence in the areas of social rights covered by the Charter, as for Article 3 of the same Protocol. The Committee of Experts clarified that, for the purpose of collective complaints, 'representativeness' is to be intended as 'an autonomous concept ... not identical to the national notion'. In this case, a Norwegian organisation representing small and medium enterprises, lodged a complaint because it was denied the fundamental right to organise. The Committee declared it admissible not so much on the account of the number of members associated with the complainant, rather on the recognition of its 'real, active and independent' role.[43]

The discussion on accession to the ESC, as well as to the ECHR, found new energy in the aftermath of the crisis and has been addressed in research promoted by the EP.[44] Several collective complaints were, in fact, initiated by trade unions and other organisations in countries most affected by austerity measures, thus proving the significance of parallel routes to follow for the protection of fundamental social rights.

In the adoption and the improvement of social policies, the so-called 'horizontal' clauses set out in Articles 8 and 9 TFEU, recalled above, must apply. However, the implications rising from the joint interpretation of all such sources has not been put in action on the occasion of approving austerity measures, during different phases of the crisis. National laws adopted in compliance with MoUs in bailout countries have been challenged, referring to the violation of standards in international sources, rather than to EU primary and secondary law. The latter challenges proved, in fact, more controversial, because of the uncertain legal status of MoUs as European acts and, consequently, for their enforceability by the CJEU.

despite its programmatic function. The aims to be pursued must be clearly defined by competent authorities.

43 Complaint No. 103/2013, points 13 and 14.

44 O. De Schutter, *The European Social Charter in the Context of Implementation of the EU Charter of Fundamental Rights*, EP 2016, a study promoted by the Policy Department, Citizens' Rights and Constitutional Affairs, PE 536.488.

Article 152 TFEU – a novelty introduced in the Lisbon Treaty – includes the precious heritage of the 'European social dialogue'. This expression, created by Jacques Delors in 1985, is meant to define the relationship of reciprocal consultation among European organisations of employers and workers, which in the past resulted in the adoption of common opinions and joint policy statements. Social dialogue is now widespread and more articulated. References have been made before to sector European agreements. Furthermore, over the years social partners have signed cross-industry agreements[45] and a number of joint texts. The latter address specific issues, and take the form of auspices and commitments, which have little impact on law-makers, but signify the reach of consensus among representative organisations.

Article 152 introduces the 'Tripartite Social Summit for Growth and Employment', where the social partners are endowed with consultative prerogatives only. The Summit meets twice, first in the so-called Spring Council and then again in the Fall.

To the emphasis already put on the diversity of national systems and on the autonomy of social partners, in respect of the principle of subsidiarity, we can add that Article 152 assigns to organisations representing workers and employers at European level a quasi-public role. However, social partners during trilateral meetings are not fully included in the decision-making processes because they are not fully legitimated to take final decisions.

It is worth recalling that the Treaty of Lisbon (Article 16 paragraph 6 TEU), expressly provides that the Council meets in different formations. The Council in this way acquires a well-defined institutional status within the limits of European law (Articles 235 and 236 TFEU), without sacrificing certain informal elements which, since the beginning, characterised its own functioning. It is not a coincidence that the involvement of social partners, granted through their consultation during the already mentioned trilateral social meeting, happened in an informal venue, certainly not like the meetings of the Council where the relevant economic decisions are taken.

Taking into account this discrepancy among different Council's configurations and being aware of the harsh criticism raised by social partners during the crisis, this practice should be changing. In the urgency of

[45] European Commission, Employment, Social Affairs and Inclusion, *Cross-industry Social Dialogue Database Telework* (2002), *Stress at Work, Harassment and Violence at Work* (2007) *and Inclusive Labour Market* (2010).

adopting more incisive measures, the Commission has proposed, as part of the reform of economic governance, the consultation of social partners even before Council's meetings dealing with economic and financial matters. This auspice was in the agenda set by the President of the Commission, Juncker, who promised to re-visit social dialogue.[46]

Notwithstanding the criticism of commentators with regard to the scarce relevance of the amendments brought about by the Treaty of Lisbon and, more broadly, on the weak potentialities of a social market economy,[47] we must start from the modifications introduced in the Treaties over the years, in order to interpret new tendencies of social policies and to evaluate the obligations that EU law addresses to national administrations. The path to follow is one of a coherent direction, which should guide all the actors performing on the stage of the play. The metaphor of a theatre, mentioned above to recall the institutional framework within which reforms are enhanced, helps in visualising a public space of deliberations and, at times, of tough confrontation.

However, messages coming from a public space do not always reach the audience uniformly and reassuringly. This is what happened, for instance, in the representation of an economic and financial crisis of serious relevance that, to stay in the theatrical metaphor, resulted in too rapid changes of the background within the European stage and in a difficult research of effective measures to deal with it. The overall coherence of the directorship risks being lost and so does the appeal of the text addressed to the audience.

Employment and social policies are, certainly not unexpectedly, an integral part of the strategies to cope with the crisis. The social climate is such to contribute to increasing the 'fear of Europe' among citizens, a fear which is fuelled by the references, instrumentally made in domestic politics, to the obligations imposed by the EU. All such obligations are, in fact, the outcome of political negotiations frequently made at intergovernmental level, rather than within the European institutions.[48]

[46] One outcome of this promise is: Council Decision (EU) 2016/1859 of 13 October 2016 on the Tripartite Social Summit for Growth and Employment and repealing Decision 2003/174 EC.

[47] Fritz W. Scharpf, 'The asymmetry of European integration, or why the EU cannot be a "social market economy"', *Socio-Economic Review*, 8 (2010), 211–50; C. Joerges and F. Rödl, '"Social Market Economy" as Europe's social model?', EUI Working Paper Law 8/2004.

[48] S. Fabbrini, *Which European Union? Europe after the Euro Crisis* (Cambridge University Press 2015).

2.1 The European Semester and the Role of the Employment and Social Affairs Council

Answers to the crisis that governments have to offer as part of the obligations rising from membership of the EU require the adoption of coordinated measures of political economy, in order to ensure stability and re-launch growth and employment. During the so-called European Semester, a cycle started in 2011, in order to simplify previous procedures, specific tasks are required to Member States with regard to fiscal policies and plans for the consolidation of public debt.

The European Semester was formalised through Regulation 1175/2011 belonging to the so-called Six-Pack.[49] In January the overall picture of economic priorities is set and the Annual Growth Survey is presented, where measures to tackle recovery are put forward, having as priorities growth and employment. This Survey is accompanied by the Alert Mechanism Report, which serves the purpose to identify imbalances and address them to each country.

The Joint Employment Report is also attached to the Survey and supplemented by the points of view expressed in official documents by all social partners. In April, National Reforms Programs (NRP), framed within the agenda of Europe 2020, are presented together with Stability and Convergence Programmes, the latter requested by the reformed Stability and Growth Pact.[50] Such programmes include references to labour and social policies and should not have a mere aspirational value, as has happened in employment policies enforced under the so-called OMC, designed in 2000 in the context of the Strategy initiated in Lisbon.[51] NRPs are subject to close evaluation, in order to address each Member State on specific grounds, notwithstanding respect for the sovereignty of national parliaments.

On this basis, the Commission presents country-specific recommendations in May, in view of the Council's adoption in June. However, in

[49] Regulation (EU) No. 1175/2011 of the European Parliament and of the Council of 16 November 2011 [2011] OJ L306/12. The Six-Pack is a set of five Regulations and one Directive aimed at strengthening the preventive and corrective arms of the Stability and Growth Pact. The latter was also reinforced by the Two-Pack, which came into force in 2013 and added further monitoring systems for countries of the Euro area in order to improve budgetary surveillance and coordination.

[50] Regulation (EU) No. 1175/2011 of the European Parliament and of the Council, of 16 November 2011 amending Council Regulation (EC) No. 1466/97 on the strengthening of the surveillance of budgetary positions and the surveillance and coordination of economic policies.

[51] See Chapter 2.

2015 the May deadline was brought forward to February, in order to allow more time and a more detailed scrutiny. To complete the picture of this calendar of commitments, euro area countries are required to submit draft budget plans by 15 October, in view of the final adoption by 31 December.

This strict and intense plan of commitments, implying incumbent obligations on Member States, may very well justify an increasing 'fear of Europe'. Policies of fiscal consolidation, imposed on countries with a view to reducing public debts, had in some cases very negative implications for employment and did not stimulate growth. Furthermore, the lack of attention in promoting wage increases exacerbated problems related to so-called 'working poors' and aggravated income inequalities.

Research shows the negative impact of all this on social development. One outcome is the appearance of new social divides among the weakest groups in society, such as the elderly and the young. The latter are the ones who suffered most, as data on the rising number of young people not in employment, education or training (the acronym widely used is NEET) in all twenty-eight countries show very clearly.[52]

In the attempt to facilitate coordination of policies and set targets within specific deadlines, the European Semester has progressively ignored the involvement of social partners. The strengthened economic governance programme, part of the Stability and Growth Pact, incorporates the Macroeconomic Imbalance Procedure, in order to detect problems at an early stage. The instrument adopted by the Commission is the Alert Mechanism Report, which, at the beginning of the fourth European Semester in November 2013, brought the Commission to enforce the screening of all Member States, on the basis of a scoreboard of indicators.[53] But social rights were not part of that assessment, despite the Commission's declared intention to strengthen the social dimension of economic governance.

In a resolution, followed by specific Recommendations to the Council,[54] the EP acknowledged critically its own limited involvement and developed a detailed critique of the European Semester. The EP

[52] Z. Darvas and O. Tschekassin, *Poor and Under Pressure: The Social Impact of Europe's Fiscal Consolidation*, Bruegel Policy contribution (2015), 4, March 2015.

[53] See ec.europa.eu/economy_finance/publications/occasional_paper/2012/pdf/ocp92_en.pdf.

[54] European Parliament resolution of 25 February 2014 on the European Semester for economic policy coordination: Employment and Social Aspects in the Annual Growth Survey 2014 (2013/2158(INI)).

argued that social indicators, unlike in the Macroeconomic Imbalance Procedure scoreboard, are not binding. They are inadequate, in particular with regard to inequalities due to lowering wages and in-job poverty. Wage increases are not sufficiently encouraged, despite the beneficial impact they could have in increasing propensity to spending.[55]

The EP also underlined a critical unbalance and lack of coordination among the Economic and Financial Affairs Council (Ecofin), on the one hand, and Employment and social affairs council meetings, on the other. The lack of coordination among different configurations of the Council is stigmatised as a consequence of the exceedingly strong position assigned to the Commission, described as the leading actor in running the show of the European Semester.

The criticism raised by the European Trade Union Confederation (ETUC) runs along similar lines.[56] Furthermore, a comprehensive study[57] shows the contradictions emerging from the implementation of austerity measures. The largest cuts in social spending took place in countries with a high risk of poverty and social exclusion. Limitations put on public spending prevailed on measures for social inclusion and no attention was paid to the increasing level of poverty among working people. All these missed opportunities in further enhancing social law demonstrate that growing inequalities among weak groups in the labour market – rather than inclusion and enhanced protection – are the prevailing outcomes of current economic governance.

The point to be made is whether and how the very complex machinery, which supports the European Semester, should become compatible with social dialogue, so as to allow for consultation and involvement of representative organisations and bring forward themes related to social justice and social protection. So far, the only visible sign of change is the simultaneous publication by the Commission of the annual growth survey, the draft Joint Employment Report and the Alert Mechanism Report, all delivered in November 2014. The Commission then addressed to the Council an economic surveillance package in February 2015, in order to clarify all the steps of the Macroeconomic Imbalance Procedure for specific countries. This procedure continues to be implemented every

[55] See, for example, 'Building growth: country-specific recommendations' (Commission Press Release 2014), IP/14/623, 6 February 2014.

[56] See www.etuc.org/documents/etuc-position-european-commission-communication-strengthening-social-dimension-economic#.U2-wFyidSbk.

[57] ETUI, *Benchmarking Working Europe 2014* (Brussels: ETUI 2014).

year and specific in-depth reviews are carried on for countries experiencing economic imbalances.[58]

2.2 *The Euro Plus Pact: Wage Moderation and Decentralised Bargaining*

The European Council of 24 and 25 March 2011 will be remembered as a watershed in the economic governance of the EU, with the adoption of the Euro Plus Pact, binding for Member States – the ones in the Eurozone and some others that take part in it – with regard to the concrete actions to be adopted during the year, in the context of stronger coordination. Even if the choice of the actions to be adopted remains squarely within the discretion of national parliaments, the supranational assessment, carried out every year, should not give much space to defaulting states.

We can look, in particular, at the Conclusions adopted on 24 and 25 March 2011 and at Annex I, dealing, among other things, with pay policies and productivity. A scrupulous attitude of the Council goes as far as suggesting a periodical assessment of unit labour costs in national economies in their entirety and for large sectors of the economy. The growing of competitiveness cannot be separated, in the indications of the Council, from the revision of systems of wage setting.

One feature to review is the excessive centralisation of collective bargaining, which should be avoided; indexation mechanisms too should be excluded. Bargaining should typically take place at a decentralised level. These safeguards also concern, as it is easy to imagine, the public sector.[59] The Greek crisis, which burst in the summer of 2011, showed all these contradictions and proved that institutional delays of the EU institutions in denouncing the incorrect functioning of collective bargaining and excesses in public spending could have avoided, at least in part, the dramatic consequences that hit the country.

The nature of sanctions to be inflicted is not clear, following the pressing indications coming from the Euro Plus Pact. The call to respect national traditions and the autonomy of collective bargaining, included in Annex I, soon appeared insufficient and was not accompanied by other and more visible measures to support the actions of social partners. The emphasis put on policies of wage moderation and on the responsibility of

[58] Social agenda No. 40, April 2015 – EU economic policy in the making (April 2015).

[59] C. Barnard, 'The financial crisis and the Euro Plus Pact: a labour lawyer's perspective', *International Law Journal*, 41 (2012), 98 ff.

social partners fuelled even more the fear of Europe, in the absence of clearer strategic plans about growth and employment policies.

All the more so in the case of Italy – not to become a bailout country – since the invitation to improve competitiveness and decentralise collective bargaining with regard to salaries was contained in a letter delivered in August 2011 by the ECB. The letter, by all means an anomalous source, was exposed to strong instrumental attitudes in the Italian discussions preceding the reform of the labour market, because of an allegedly excessive emphasis put on the urgency to reform dismissal law. In that informal document addressed to Italy – to be deemed morally, if not legally, binding in the delicate equilibrium created during the explosion of the crisis – the ECB proposed a series of measures without preferring any of them and suggesting the necessity to combine interventions on various directions.[60]

With regard to the Euro Plus Pact, we can maintain that the urgent measures to be adopted with regard to wage policies, to simplify them and orientate them towards the improvement of productivity, did not produce the expected outcomes. A gap persists between economic and monetary policies on the one hand and social policies on the other, exactly at a time when European citizens perceive dramatically the absence of political choices favouring growth and employment. Wage policies, as indicated earlier, are a crucial element of current monitoring exercised by EU institutions, albeit in a still unsatisfactory way.

It is now time to proceed, even if in general terms, with references to the measures the EU adopted, coping with the crisis, in order to better explain where the 'fear of Europe' is generated.

2.3 *The ESM: Answers from Constitutional Courts and the CJEU*

The harshening of the Greek crisis, during the summer of 2011, made the recourse to the European Financial Stability Facility (EFSF) more pressing.[61] This mechanism found its place within the Luxembourg legal system and was created on 7 June 2010 through a Decision of the sixteen States of the Euro group, which was followed by the signature of the EFSF framework agreement on the same day and modified on 21 July 2011. The EFSF acted in

60 A. Lo Faro, 'Italian labour law in recession: legislative actions and judicial reactions', *European Journal of Social Law*, 1 (2014), 75.

61 Decisions of the Representatives of the Government of the Euro Area Member States Meeting within the Council of the EU, ECOFIN, 9 May 2010. Doc. No. 9614/10.

the transitional phase, namely while awaiting the completion of the setting up of the ESM, in agreement with the states of the Eurozone, in order to calm down the crisis through precautionary measures, loans and other forms of support.

Temporary measures to support Member States, launched in the aftermath of the crisis, were comprised within the ESM. This step, which is central for the relations between Member States and European institutions, required a modification of Article 136 TFEU, which concentrates on measures to improve the functioning of the Economic and Monetary Union. The European Council approved this amendment, to be implemented through the signature of a new Treaty.[62]

Under ESM the mobilisation of funding 'to provide stability support' can imply, for countries undergoing serious financial problems, the entering into 'agreements or arrangements with ESM members, financial institutions or other third parties' (Article 3). Whenever a decision is reached, a MoU is signed, reflecting the severity of each case and the measures to be adopted (Article 13.3). These new sources, still to be framed within a clear legal status, have raised criticism and given rise to complaints addressed to international organisations and to the CJEU.

The procedure to grant stability support is initiated by Member States. The chairperson of the board, on receipt of the request, involves the European Commission and the ECB, in order to evaluate it and assess all connected risks. If a positive decision is reached, the International Monetary Fund (IMF) enters the scene 'wherever possible' and takes part in the negotiations with the Member State concerned, in view of reaching a MoU, reflecting the severity of the case and the measures to be adopted (Article 13.3).

The presence of the IMF does not entirely detach the procedure from its European roots, since it is established that a 'MoU shall be fully consistent with the measures of economic policy coordination provided for in the TFEU, in particular with any act of European Union law, including any opinion, warning, recommendation or decision addressed to the ESM Member concerned'. Furthermore, the signature of the agreement is the task of the Commission, on behalf of the ESM (Article 13.4). However, the presence of the IMF adds an institutional dimension which is not only

[62] The treaty to create a European Stability Mechanism (ESM) was signed on 2 February 2012. The negotiation of the ESM was accompanied by the amendment of Article 136 TFEU, through Council Decision of 25 March 2011 (2011/199/EU) OJ L91/1, with an explicit authorisation to grant financial assistance to Eurozone Member States.

symbolically relevant, since it directly affects the balance of powers among negotiators.

It is by all means difficult to detect the status of a MoU within the framework of EU law. The origin of the ESM is, after all, to be found in an amendment to Article 136 TFEU. It consisted in a new section added to it, following a simplified decision within the European Council.

Precisely this latter amendment to the Treaty has been at the origin of a German Constitutional Court's ruling, based on the potential attack to statehood and the consequent restriction of sovereignty caused by the signing of an international treaty such as the one establishing ESM.[63] As long as Germany's payment obligations are kept within the initially agreed contribution – the Federal Constitutional Court has argued – the ESM can function properly, in parallel with EU primary law, given the urgency to enforce common strategies within the EU.

This answer, given in an interim judgment, delivered on 12 September 2012, implied the refusal to issue a temporary injunction against the ratification of the Treaty. In its final judgment on the same issue, delivered on 18 March 2014, the German Constitutional Court confirmed its view, indicating the prevailing role of parliamentary scrutiny over government decisions.[64]

On 12 July 2012, the Estonian Supreme Court delivered a judgment in which ESM, and in particular Article 4(4) dealing with urgent financial assistance, was at stake. The 'emergency voting procedure' is supported by 85 per cent of the votes cast when a serious threat to the stability of the euro area is foreseen. Hence, the Estonian Court had to balance this measure against constitutional values. It argued for the inclusion of financial stability among national constitutional values and it confirmed a notion of solidarity among Eurozone Member States.[65]

Growing contradictions are generated by the fact that solidarity among euro area countries is not embedded within EU primary law, but subject to negotiations and to intergovernmental compromises. In drafting the amendment to Article 136 TFEU careful consideration was given to the 'no bail-out clause' dealt with in Article 125 TFEU. Eurozone countries had to be kept within a scheme of action which would enhance solidarity

[63] F. Schorkopf, 'Start the engines. Comment on the ESM-judgment of the German Federal Constitutional Court of 12 September 2012', *Maastricht Journal of European and Comparative Law*, 19 (2012), 554 ff.

[64] *14 German Law Journal*, 1 (2013), a special issue dedicated to these decisions.

[65] Comments in F. Fabbrini, *Economic Governance in Europe: Comparative Paradoxes and Constitutional Challenges* (Oxford University Press 2016), 69 ff.

towards the ones most severely hit by the crisis, without creating 'incentives to moral hazard . . . relying on the support of other Member States, or of the Union'.[66]

The translation of solidarity into concrete measures to help people, as well as Member States, is entrusted to sources – such as MoUs – which are not institutionally designed to include collective actors representing large organised interests. This deficiency brought several organisations to lodge complaints with international bodies different from EU institutions.[67]

In such a scheme, the real danger is to detach national systems of collective bargaining and other forms of consensus building institutions embedded in national traditions, without providing a supranational body in which collective deliberations can be taken, while consulting legitimate representatives of the interests under discussion. MoUs are hybrid sources, generated by a treaty. The latter departs from the European method, even though pursuing objectives which should be common for the EU as a whole.[68]

This controversial subject matter is now at the core of a CJEU's ruling, following a preliminary reference from Romania. The Court acknowledges that a MoU 'is based in law on Article 143 TFEU, which gives the Union the power to grant mutual assistance to a Member State'. Hence, as 'an act whose legal basis lies in the provisions of EU law [it] constitutes

[66] R. Cisotta, 'Financial stability and the reconstruction of the EU legal order in the aftermath of the crisis', in proceedings of the European Central Bank (ECB) Legal Conference 2015 'From Monetary Union to Banking Union, on the way to Capital Markets Union – New opportunities for European integration', ECB publication, 287, www.ecb.europa.eu/pub/pdf/other/frommonetaryuniontobankingunion201512.en.pdf.

[67] ILO Committee on Freedom of Association, Case No. 2820 (Greece), complaint brought in 2010 by several Greek unions (Greek General Confederation of Labour – GSEE, Civil Servants' Confederation – ADEDY, General Federation of Employees of the National Electric Power Corporation – GENOP-DEI-KIE, and Greek Federation of Private Employees – OIYE), supported by the International Trade Union Confederation (ITUC), denouncing the austerity measures taken by the Greek government, under pressure after the deliberation of European institutions and the IMF, complaint also to Council of Europe (see the Report No. 365, in which the committee requests to be kept informed of development, November 2012, www.ilo.org/dyn/normlex/en/f?p=1000:50002:0::NO:50002:P50002_COMPLAINT_TEXT_ID:3087085).

[68] The CJEU decided it was manifestly incompetent in Case C-128/12, Order of the Court (Sixth Chamber) of 7 March 2013, *Sindicato dos Bancários do Norte and Others* v. *BPN – Banco Português de Negócios SA*, and in Case C-264/12, Order of 26 June 2014. MoUs are indicated as justiciable sources by the EP: *Report on the Enquiry on the Role and Operations of the Troika (ECB, Commission and IMF) with regard to the euro area programme countries*, www.europarl.europa.eu/sides/getDoc.do?pubRef=-//EP//TEXT+REPORT+A7-2014-0149+0+DOC+XML+V0//EN. See also C. Kilpatrick, 'Are the bail-outs immune to EU social challenge because they are not EU law?', *Europe Constitutional Law Review*, 10 (2014), 393.

an act of an EU institution within the meaning of Article 267 (b) TFEU'.[69] This judgment goes beyond a formalistic reading of the law and captures the concrete function of a MoU. The latter is an agreement between EU institutions and a Member State, based on an economic programme, which represents the precondition to receive medium-term financial assistance outside the Eurozone. It is correct to attach to this source a precise function among the many resources set in action by the crisis and to acknowledge that MoUs are signed by EU institutions, which are due to comply with the rule of law and protect fundamental rights.

This latest decision must be framed within a complex discussion, in which the CJEU had already raised its voice. In *Pringle*[70] the CJEU had to consider a reference for a preliminary ruling lodged by the Irish Supreme Court in proceedings brought by a member of the Irish Parliament against the Irish government, arguing that Decision 2011/199 adopted to amend Article 136 TFEU would be unlawful and that in signing the Treaty establishing the ESM Ireland would create a situation of incompatibility with its membership of the EU. This lengthy and highly technical judgment is significant in many respects, which cannot be fully analysed here.

One point to highlight in *Pringle* has to do with the interpretation the Court offers of its own jurisdiction. The Court frames the ESM within the scheme of economic policies as matters of common interest provided for in the Treaty (Articles 120 ff, and in particular 123 to 125, TFEU), subject to coordination in view of reaching the objectives set in Article 3 TEU. Preventive interventions, already provided for in the TFEU, are now entwined with ESM. The latter does not enter monetary policies, but only pursues 'the management of financial crisis which, notwithstanding such preventive action as might have been taken, might nonetheless arise'.[71] The Court thus accomplishes its own function, arguing on the compatibility of ESM with both the objectives set out in the TEU and the regulatory technique enshrined in the TFEU with regard to economic and monetary policies and interprets stability as an absolute priority. It

[69] Case C-258/14, *Eugenia Florescu and Others* v. *Casa Județeană de Pensii Sibiu and Others*, Judgment of the Court (Grand Chamber) of 13 June 2017, Request for a preliminary ruling from the Curtea de Apel Alba Iuliaat, paragraph 35.

[70] Case C-370/12, *Thomas Pringle* v. *Government of Ireland, Ireland and The Attorney General*. Judgment of 27 November 2012. See *The ESM Before the Court, German Law Journal*, Special Section, XIV (2013) 1–190. B. De Witte and T. Beukers, 'The Court of Justice approves the creation of the European Stability Mechanism outside the EU legal order: Pringle', *Common Market Law Review*, 50 (2013), 805 ff.

[71] *Pringle*, supra n. 70, at 59.

has been maintained that in *Pringle* the Court is implicitly assuming that EU competences in economic policies can be expanded at the detriment of Member States. This reading of the case runs parallel to the interpretation that, during the crisis, Article 136 TFEU has been the legal basis for actions aiming at closer coordination of economic policies.[72]

What the Court did not do in *Pringle* was to interpret MoUs as instruments connected with the broad economic policies guidelines, which are part of EU law. As sources inherent to the ESM Treaty, they represent the long arm of the three institutions – the Commission, the ECB and the IMF – which descend into national grounds. This position is clarified in *Florescu*, in which the issue at stake was the adoption of legislation prohibiting the combination of public sector retirement pension with income from other activities carried out in public institutions, if the amount of the pension exceeds the amount of the average gross national salary, on the basis of which the Romanian social security budget was drawn up.[73] The Court points to the discretion of national legislators in adopting measures, which are, nevertheless, connected with the obligations subscribed in MoUs.

In this scenario the point of view of social law, strictly connected with priorities to be set in national economic policies, could be marginalised, together with the organisations representing collective interests. The latter are, on some occasions, asked to become the facilitators of urgent and difficult choices to be made, without having a voice in economic governance. A regulatory technique, similar to the one enshrined in the TFEU for the adoption of social policies (Article 154 ff.), whereby social partners must be consulted and given the opportunity to put forward proposals, is still missing.

In that framework, the Commission 'shall consult management and labour on the possible direction of Union action' (Article 154.2) and, should the action become advisable, 'shall consult management and labour on the content of the envisaged proposal' (Article 154.3). These procedural steps aim at the inclusion of social partners within the institutional law-making, notwithstanding the differences of all actors involved. This source

[72] Cisotta, 'Financial stability', supra n. 66, 285 ff.

[73] On 22 March 2017, the Italian Constitutional Court delivered a judgment (124/2017) in which it held constitutional a budget law imposing maximum limit on remunerations and pensions out of public funds. The English translation is at www.cortecostituzionale.it/documenti/download/doc/recent_judgments/S_124_2017_EN.pdf. It is noteworthy that even a non-bailout country should face financial constraints in fields similarly affected by public spending.

of inspiration, which has also been at the origin of important experiments in adopting social law Directives, could be considered for future developments of the European social law method and adapted to other areas of economic governance.

2.4 *The Fiscal Compact*

In discussing fiscal policies the first reference must be made to the Stability and Growth Pact (SGP), dating back to 1992 and functional in the take-off of the Economic and Monetary Union (EMU) in the Maastricht Treaty. The two arms of SGP, a preventive and a corrective one, as they are referred to, were designed to become instrumental in reaching the objectives of the Pact. This language is in itself explanatory of the overall philosophy inspiring the Pact, originally thought of as complementary to EMU, and then caught in between the many emergencies caused by the crisis. Several changes have occurred over the years. Mention has already been made of the Six-Pack and the Two-Pack, which entered into force respectively in 2011 and 2013.

Among all these initiatives attention should also be paid to the Pact for Growth and Employment, also defined as the Growth Compact,[74] approved at the European Council of 28 and 29 June 2012. This additional initiative was driven by the intention to reorganise a series of already existing proposals and to prioritise the use of temporary financing of the most urgent measures – including measures to favour youth employment – through the European Social Fund.

It is interesting to contextualise the timing of these initiatives, since the Commission made the EU Cohesion policy budget for the years 2007–2013 available to support growth and in particular to address very critical matters, such as youth unemployment. The idea was to target in more direct and efficient ways recourse to EU structural funds and to encourage Member States whose budgets were in a critical state to use these resources, by reducing their co-financing quotas. The necessary amendments to the budget were pivotal to the overall reform of the EU budget for the years 2014–2020 and to increased coordination with policies indicated in Europe 2020.

Another contribution to this insistent series of innovations is an intergovernmental Treaty, referred to as the 'Fiscal Compact', signed on 2 March

[74] European Commission, *Implementation of the Compact for Growth and Jobs*, Report to the European Council, 18–19 October 2012.

2012, with the opt-out of the United Kingdom and of the Czech Republic.[75] The aim of a stronger preventive coordination of economic policies in the Eurozone was accompanied by the objective to pursue sustainable growth, employment, competitiveness and social cohesion. In the preamble it is clarified that 'granting of financial assistance in the framework of new programmes under the European Stability Mechanism will be conditional, as of 1 March 2013, on the ratification of this Treaty'.[76]

In reply to this, a resolution titled 'A social pact for Europe' was adopted by the executive committee of the European Confederation of trade unions in June 2012. In this critical document, the emphasis is on collective bargaining and social dialogue, essential instruments to redistribute the burdens in implementing a new phase of the economic governance. This document ended up having a mere declaratory effect and was not followed by immediate responses from the European institutions.

The Fiscal Compact eluded all forms of consultation with the social partners. The lack of social consensus was aggravated by the fact that the transposition of the SGP into national legal systems, because of the continuing and pervasive effects of the crisis, implied stricter mechanisms of compliance, subject to constant evaluation.

Dilemmas attached to the implementation of the Fiscal Compact are still unsolved. In order to foster long-term growth, fiscal policies should not be an impediment to the enhancement of structural reforms. Empirical studies do not provide evidence of measurable costs for specific reforms. For example, active labour market policies require short-term budget allocations, whereas clearer assessments have been made for long-term pension reforms.

Hence, it is maintained that there is a need to conduct further research in view of introducing flexibility into the rigid scheme of fiscal policies and monitoring the enforcement of reforms, in order to avoid that they remain mere announcements. It has also been observed that public investment declined in countries hit by the crisis and that efforts should be made to start pan-European public infrastructures.[77] ETUC elaborates criticism along similar lines, arguing for the urgent need to boost public investment in order to provide high quality public services.[78]

[75] Treaty on Stability, Coordination and Governance in the Economic and Monetary Union, 2, 2012.

[76] S. Fabbrini, *Which European Union*, supra n. 48, 54 ff.

[77] L. Eyraud and T. Wu, 'Playing by the rules: reforming fiscal governance in Europe', IMF Working Paper 15/67, March 2015, 23–5.

[78] ETUC Position on the Annual Growth Survey 2016, delivered on 28–9 October 2015.

2.5 *Fiscal Councils and the European Fiscal Board*

An additional side of the complex machinery put in place by EU fiscal measures has to do with the creation of the so-called fiscal councils, rooted in national administrations and independent from national parliaments. The legal basis for such Independent Fiscal Institutions (IFI) is in Directive 2011/85/EU, part of the Six-Pack and binding for all Member States except the United Kingdom, and in the Two-Pack Regulation (EU) 473/2013, binding on Eurozone countries only.[79]

In 2015, an EU Independent Fiscal Councils Network was created, in order to facilitate exchanges and promote coordination of national measures, despite the lack of specific measures in EU law. The only indirect reference is in Article 6 of Directive 2011/85, where collaboration with the Commission in the course of the European Semester is envisaged, as part of the monitoring compliance mechanisms, with 'independent bodies or bodies endowed with fiscal autonomy vis-à-vis the fiscal authorities of the member States'. Great emphasis is put on fiscal councils as enablers of virtuous and transparent practices in national parliaments. Their independence should foster well-balanced choices and combine compliance of budget constraints with the assessment of essential priorities.

One further novelty is the European Fiscal Board (EFB), an independent advisory body regulated by Commission's Decision (EU) 2015/1937, adopted on 21 October 2015 as a follow-up to the Five Presidents' Report on 'Completing Europe's Economic and Monetary Union'.[80]

A prolonged exacerbated crisis within the EU complicated the evaluation of all such mechanisms and institutions. Proposals put forward by the President of the Commission in the 'Investment Plan for Europe', the so-called 'Juncker plan' approved in June 2015, entail synergies between public and private investments. The new European Fund for Strategic Investments (EFSI) should trigger new initiatives. One of the criticisms addressed to this plan, apart from its very slow implementation, is that EFSI mainly reproduces projects of the European

[79] C. Fasone and D. Fromage, 'Fiscal councils: threat or opportunity in the post-crisis economic and monetary union?', in L. Daniele, P. Simone, and R. Cisotta (eds.), *Democracy in the EMU in the Aftermath of the Crisis* (Vienna-Turin: Springer–Giappichelli 2017), 161 ff.

[80] European Commission, *Five Presidents' Report: Completing Europe's Economic and Monetary Union*, 2015, 14, 22, annex 3, available at ec.europa.eu/priorities/economic-monetary-union/docs/5-presidents-report_en.pdf.

Investment Bank (EIB), whereas it should foster financing of new projects.[81]

Juncker's political commitments put forward when he took office as President of the Commission on 1 November 2014, included the return to social dialogue. In fact, in March 2015 the social partners were brought together in a high level meeting, with the aim of starting a new phase characterised by deeper involvement of management and labour in decision-making, including consultation within the scheme of the European Semester.[82] The follow-up to that meeting is not so visible yet, but the role of social partners in putting forward strategies to compensate the effects of the crisis should not be underestimated.

The construction of an integrated Europe of fiscal policies, so much needed to accompany and improve EMU, emerges from the crisis as an intergovernmental project, distant from the classic European method. This choice can, in the long run, marginalise the European Parliament and delegitimise European institutions. This subtle and yet persistent de-politicisation of European policies explains where the 'fear of Europe' comes from and how arduous it is to dissolve the fear into more promising visions of the future.[83]

2.6 *The Intuitions of the Barca Report: Social Cohesion and Partnership Agreements*

I have previously underlined the urgency to flank austerity measures with choices more attentive to social and employment policies. To counterbalance negative outcomes of the crisis it proved indispensable to provide financial support to all such policies and to empower all actors involved.

A plan to cope with the crisis, presented in 2008 by the Commission, had, on the one hand, the objective to reinvigorate the demand-side through financial incentives, while complying with the SGP. On the other hand, it included structural initiatives to support employment, through the simplification of criteria to access the European Social Fund, for instance increasing quotas of funding to be anticipated to Member

[81] This is the opinion expressed by G. Claeys and A. Leandro, 'The Juncker plan needs to be turned on its head', 8 June 2016, bruegel.org/2016/06/the-juncker-plan-needs-to-be-turned-on-its-head/.

[82] See European Commission, *New Start for Social Dialogue. One Year On*, Brussels 16 March 2016.

[83] Tuori and Tuori, supra n. 16, 211–13.

States.[84] A parallel initiative, which was later on confirmed in the Small Business Act,[85] facilitated the access to credit for small and medium enterprises, in continuity with other measures to cope with the crisis in the short term, allowing for derogations to the rules on state aids.[86]

These initiatives address the necessity not to distort competition in the internal market through economic aid to national undertakings. On the other hand, the inadequacy of budget lines to support employment policies must be acknowledged through reinvigorated recourse to the European Social Fund and other structural funds.

The understanding on how to have access to resources in an efficient manner comes from the Barca Report.[87] This very dense and well-argued document, based on an accurate investigation, identified the numerous shortcomings of Member States in the deployment of structural funds and the urgency to define in a clear way the interplay between different levels of the administrations involved.

The translation into operative terms of the ideas included in the Barca Report can be found in the package of proposals the Commission presented on 6 October 2011,[88] aiming at legislative measures that would link in a more stringent way financial support with the priorities set in the Europe 2020 strategy.

Policies of social cohesion should, in the vision of the Report, intersect employment policies through a more central role given to subnational entities. Partnership agreements, to be concluded between the Commission and Member States, should be planned around specific tasks, in order to assess *ex ante* the ability of administrations in acceding to funds and measure *ex post* the results achieved. In particular, for defaulting Member States sanctions should be provided, escalating from the suspension of the financing to their complete cancellation.

[84] COM (2008) 800 final, 26 November 2008.

[85] Communication from the Commission to the Council, the European Parliament, the European economic and social committee and the committee of the regions, *Think small first. A small business act for Europe*, COM (2008) 394 final, Brussels 25 June 2008. As part of the proposals put forward in the Monti Report and transferred into the Single Market Act, it applies to companies with fewer than 250 employees.

[86] Communication from the Commission to the Council, to the European Parliament, to the Committee of the Regions and to the European and Social Committee, *An action plan to improve access to finance for SMEs*, COM (2011) 870 final, 7 December 2011.

[87] F. Barca, *An agenda for a reformed cohesion policy prepared at the request of D. Hubner Commissioner for regional policy*, April 2009.

[88] European Commission, *Cohesion Policy 2014–2020. Investing in Growth and Jobs* (Luxembourg 2011).

The language adopted in the Barca Report is a sophisticated one, inspired by theories of multilevel governance and guided by the principle of subsidiarity in the assignment of tasks to different institutional actors. The scheme is to enhance a better dialogue among Member States, regions and European institutions in a long-lasting learning process. The 'place-based approach' is particularly suitable for states with a long tradition in regional policy and should introduce efficiency and coordination with national development policies.

Following the Report's policy recommendations, the Commission suggested the adoption of a code of conduct, including clear obligations for all partners involved, so that to achieve the formal signature of partnership agreements, which would bind actors at sub-national levels, while keeping Member States responsible for the implementation of the same. Following the entering into force of the regulation laying down common provisions for recourse to EU structural and investment funds,[89] the code of conduct has been adopted by the Commission as a 'delegated act', in order to facilitate the coordination of public policies.[90] Partnership agreements and programmes should not, in fact, concern single companies, but wider communities of stakeholders with common responsibilities. Recourse to these agreements is considered mandatory for the period 2014–2020, in connection with the enforcement of Europe 2020, although the modalities for the drafting and selection of the partners are left to the discretion of Member States.

The composition of the monitoring committees, competent for setting the rules of procedure, and representative of the entities involved, makes the administrative nature of these new agreements more complex. The suggestion is to support the entities involved, including social partners, with the training necessary to learn the techniques of healthy and efficient financial management and to apply them rigorously. This step confirms once more the open process of learning, which should bind together all actors involved in building capacities and in overcoming bureaucracy.

Multilevel governance is inventive with regard to the reshuffling of sources of law. The code of conduct, adopted as a delegated act, creates the infrastructure of binding agreements built around stringent obligations

[89] Regulation (EU) 1303/2013.

[90] Commission Delegated Regulation (EU) No. 240/2014 of 7 January 2014 on the European Code of conduct on partnership in the framework of the European structural and Investment Funds and accompanying Commission staff working document, *Best practices as regards implementation of the partnership principle in the European and Investment Funds Programmes*, SWD (2013) 540 final.

for the partners, which, as we have seen, are responsible for the financial and operational management of the initiatives. This formula mixes together in an interesting way different regulatory techniques, in order to satisfy expectations and responsibilities of the entities involved at national and sub-national level. For the organisations representing employers and workers the code of conduct defines criteria of sector and cross-industry representativeness, as an additional guarantee to the binding nature of the concluded agreements and as a connection to the areas relevant for the use of the funds.

This is yet another sign of the potentialities, inherent in different EU policies, which should concretize in the inclusion of large interest organisations in deliberative processes and in empowering them for the creation of closer interactions with the addressees of the same policies.

3 Concluding Remarks

A first conclusion to be drawn is that in time of crisis integration can be strengthened making recourse to all instruments provided for in EU law, which can encourage and foster cooperation. This conclusion applies to the different geographical zones of Europe, as well as to national and supranational administrations and, even more so, to social partners. The challenges created by an on-going process of integration, such as the one that should characterise the EU, are many, exactly because there are many adaptable solutions.

A system of economic rewards, assigned on the basis of the criteria clarified in the Barca Report,[91] and the following positions adopted by the European institutions, were intended to open the way for new synergies and create realistic paths of employment creation.

This process proved to be very slow. Notably, a harsh controversy between the Commission and the EP took place over the reform of the European budget, affecting the period 2014–2020, with regard to the amount of resources to be assigned to social and cohesion policies.[92] The rationale of the programme lies, in fact, in the creation of closer connections between policies of social and territorial cohesion, on the one hand and the implementation of the 'Europe 2020' strategy, on the other. The objective to be achieved, escaping the logic of mere bureaucratic

91 Supra n. 87 and referred to in Conclusions of the informal meeting of the European Council, held on 30 January 2012.

92 On 2 December 2013 the Council adopted the EU's multiannual financial framework (MFF) for 2014–2020 (11 791/7/13).

coordination between administrations, is the growth of less developed Member States and the valorisation of economically disadvantaged geographical areas, where data on employment are the most worrying.

National regimes of solidarity cannot but open themselves to the inclusion of this novelty. Protectionism, even if exercised with regard to national systems of collective bargaining and the social guarantees stemming from them, is not an adequate solution, precisely because it goes against the stream of integration of the European single market. Accordingly, an antidote can be found in closer synergies within a multilevel legal system, with the creation of new places for negotiation treasuring in a virtuous manner the financial resources the EU provides and giving new responsibilities to social partners.

'Fear from Europe' is often the outcome of unsolved domestic contradictions, having to do with political disagreement when it comes to interpreting the obligations connected with EU membership. 'Fear of Europe' has been insinuated among citizens by the many complex amendments made to EU primary law and to the original architecture of the Treaties. Both fears are not unjustified and need to be taken into serious consideration by policy-makers.

The suggestion made here is to continue on the path of better synergies among existing policies, in view of sturdier political stability, which could encourage more structural reforms at an institutional level. The emphasis I put on consensus-building strategies, implying the inclusion of organisations representing collective interests in the elaboration of policies, is a reaction to the negative outcomes produced by austerity measures. It would be naive to think that this method alone answers difficult questions and it would be partial not to mention that organised groups are very often defenders of the status quo. However, the potentialities of the European social dialogue, an essential part of the European legal method, still need to be explored in view of deeper changes within the EU institutional architecture.

2

Employment Policies

1 The 'Open Method of Coordination'

In 2000 a memorable European meeting was held in Lisbon during a Portuguese Presidency of the Council.[1] That meeting is remembered, among other things, for having launched the 'Lisbon Strategy' for the enhancement of employment policies through a better coordination of existing processes, in particular through the coordination of economic, structural and social cohesion policies and the development of a knowledge economy.

Previous institutional choices – the amendments introduced with the Treaty of Amsterdam and the clear-cut positions of the European Councils of Luxembourg in 1997 and Cologne in 1999 – highlighted the weakness of the responsibilities taken in the attempt to reverse the negative direction taken by employment policies.[2]

In order to strengthen the effectiveness of an agenda so dense of programmatic lines it was decided to provide the Council with stronger coordination prerogatives, through the issuing of guidelines directed to Member States. Such guidelines, although not binding, were contemplated to be coherent and authoritative indications for domestic policy-makers. In the constructive atmosphere of the Lisbon meeting, held during a Portuguese Presidency of the Council, the formula 'Open Method of Coordination (OMC)' was invented, a formula that became very popular in subsequent years.

From a practical perspective, the guidelines of the Council should have triggered virtuous behaviours of governments, in a process of reciprocal emulation, with the objective of promoting employment policies, an area in which national sovereignty had to be kept immune from too much interference. The Treaty, in fact, does not include such subject matters among the ones to be 'harmonised', but it prefers to govern it through

[1] Lisbon European Council 23 and 24 March 2000 presidency conclusions, Lisbon strategy.

[2] S. Sciarra, 'Integration through coordination: the Employment title in the Amsterdam Treaty', *Columbia Journal of European Law*, 6 (2000), 209 ff.

coordination, which is by definition a non-binding regulatory technique. The introduction of the so-called Spring Council, to be held every year and to be dedicated to the social and economic issues connected with employment, showed, at the time, the European institutions' intention to contrast the scarce visibility of social policies and reverse a non-favourable direction. With the introduction of Article 152 TFEU, the Treaty of Lisbon institutionalised a trilateral meeting of the Council, thus recognising a formal, albeit merely consultative, role of the social partners.

From a theoretical and multidisciplinary standpoint, OMC attracted the interest of scholars who looked at all expressions of deliberative democracy, exactly when European governance was being discussed, following the publication of the Commission White Paper.[3] The opening of institutional apparatuses to the input of civil society and numerous other stakeholders pursued better transparency of decision-making processes. This was a way to react to a crisis of reliability after the negative performance of the Commission chaired by Jacques Santer, who was forced to leave office in 1999, before the end of the mandate.

Designed as a light regulatory solution, linked to a phase of transition and readjustment of European institutions, governance has ever since been cultivated as a comprehensive theory within influential academic circles, sometimes with excessive emphasis on expected outcomes, considering the impelling goals it had to achieve.[4]

Mutual learning and benchmarking were two of the keywords used to stimulate Member States towards the adoption of measures somewhat coordinated and coherent with the guidelines of the Council. Evaluating national plans presented by governments, in the absence of clear regimes of sanctions, the Council used its persuasive force, backed by the action of the Commission, which received the task of designing a system of 'social indicators' to measure employment policies and proceed with their coordination.[5]

Stable and qualified administrative apparatuses at domestic level did not always support the intergovernmental structure on which this European method was based. Hence, it proved problematic to deliver a

[3] Communication from the Commission of 25 July 2001, European governance – A white paper, COM (2001) 428 final – OJ C 287 of 12 October 2001.

[4] O. De Shutter, N. Lebessis, and J. Paterson (eds.), *Governance in the European Union*, (Luxembourg: Official Publications of the European Communities 2001).

[5] A. Atkinson, B. Cantillon, E. Marlier, and B. Nolan, *Social Indicators: The EU Social Inclusion* (Oxford University Press 2002).

concrete follow-up to the guidelines coming from the Council.[6] The almost exclusively declamatory nature of the national action plans proposed by governments had the unintended consequence of marginalising national parliaments, as well as sub-national entities and social partners.

However, the attempt to create synergies and build 'bridges' among social and employment policies was there and resulted, in a few cases, in a combination of hard and soft regulatory techniques.[7] The best examples are the Directives on part-time and fixed-term work, based on framework agreements negotiated and signed by the European social partners,[8] which were transposed into national legal systems. The expansion of flexible contracts of employment, including part-time and fixed-term, was also one of the targets included in the Council's guidelines, constantly requiring reforms of national labour markets.

An overall critical evaluation of the Lisbon Strategy is proposed in the Report drafted by a task force nominated by the chiefs of state and government and chaired by Wim Kok, a former Dutch Prime Minister.[9] Several proposals contained in that Report did not lose their topicality and are worth recalling, bearing in mind that most of the discussion of the time was centred on policies of 'flexicurity', namely a combination of flexibility and security, regarded as the necessary plan to reform the labour market and create employment.

The most preoccupying outcome of wrong employment policies – it is maintained in the Kok Report – is the segmentation of labour markets between insiders and outsiders, because this element compromises the balancing between flexibility and security. Labour should become a real option for everyone, so guaranteeing both the ageing part of the population and young people looking for a job.

[6] The Italian case is paramount of lost opportunities under the OMC. See M. Ferrera and E. Gualmini, *Rescued by Europe? Social and Labour Market Reforms in Italy from Maastricht to Berlusconi* (Amsterdam University Press 2004).

[7] C. Kilpatrick, *New EU employment governance and constitutionalism*, in G. de Bùrca and J. Scott (eds.), *Law and New Governance in the EU and US* (Oxford: Hart Publishing 2006) 131 ff.; D. Ashiagbor, *The European Employment Strategy: Labour Market Regulation and New Governance* (Oxford University Press 2005).

[8] Council Directive 97/81/EC of 15 December 1997 concerning the Framework Agreement on part-time work concluded by UNICE, CEEP and the ETUC, OJ L 014, 20/01/1998 P. 0009–0014; Council Directive 1999/70/EC of 28 June 1999 concerning the framework agreement on fixed-term work concluded by ETUC, UNICE and CEEP, OJ L 175, 10/07/1999 P. 0043–0048.

[9] *Jobs, jobs, jobs. Creating more employment in Europe*, Report of the Employment Taskforce, chaired by Wim Kok, Luxembourg 2004.

A crucial resource is education, especially for elderly workers and for the less qualified. In addition, it is necessary to close in an efficient manner the gap between offer and demand, foreseeing in advance the necessities of companies, which require specific competences. Moreover, the Report argues that it is necessary to break the vicious circle of weak investment in education through the sharing of costs with the involvement of regional and local administrative bodies.

Education becomes the key resource, if we consider that the decline in the growth of productivity was, still at the beginning of 2000, at least in part attributed to the reduction of the average working time due, among other reasons, to the expansion of part-time work. The growth of employability should have been equally effective through an education tailored to professional figures and young managers, with a stimulus towards innovation. This is why the Kok Report concentrates on the control of the concrete implementation of national plans and no longer on policies merely promised by governments.

This gap – the persistent distance between the plans presented by governments and their implementation – is still topical in current discussions on employment policies and it is still difficult to sanction efficiently delays and incomplete compliance.

Criticism on the lack of political will and on the reluctance to make employment a real priority is now framed within proposals on 'predistribution', a reformist agenda attempting, once more, to reconcile European values and objectives with concrete political choices. The conundrum is anticipation of changes in labour market reforms and the planning of training oriented to the selection of new skills, an issue that cyclically comes back to the attention of decision-makers.[10]

The Kok Report also suggested that the EU budget be reshaped, to support priorities set at Lisbon in 2000 and that budgetary incentives be introduced to encourage Member States in the achievement of the Lisbon targets. This option echoes the proposal of the Barca Report on cohesion policies, which were discussed before. This, too, continues to be a missed opportunity in contemporary discussions.

Criticism addressed to the Lisbon Strategy, presented by the task force led by Wim Kok, prompted a partial reshaping of the OMC. Changes were in line with proposals laid down in 2005 by the President of the Commission, Manuel Barroso, at the beginning of his first mandate. The

[10] C. Chwalisz and P. Diamond (eds.), *The Predistribution Agenda: Tackling Inequality and Supporting Sustainable Growth* (London-New York: Tauris 2015).

failure of this formula was in part explained because of the weakness of soft law and the lack of an incisive regime of sanctions. Another serious weakness was the absence of a real sharing of the priorities to be pursued among national governments. The practice of OMC as an intergovernmental method proved to be as uncertain in its institutional foundations as it was erratic with regard to its results.

The de-politicisation of deliberative processes, without the guide of politically responsible European institutions, did not see the rise of an enlightened bureaucracy. It weakened the competence of regulatory states in the definition of employment policies and did not improve the rescuing of the necessary finances to support them.

Years after the launching of such an experiment, it can be maintained that if closer integration had been the real objective to pursue, a system of sanctions with regard to defaulting or ineffective Member States should have been envisaged. A parallel assessment of virtuous policy-making should have been conceived, linked to selective financial support, along the lines later designed in the Barca Report.[11]

On the contrary, emphasis on soft law took the responsibility away from national administrations and undermined coordination techniques. Employment policies promoted within each national legal order should not have been separated from policies of social cohesion, with a view to reducing the gap between insiders and outsiders in labour markets. In order to achieve these objectives, strong political unity within the EU should have been a precondition for the identification of concrete priorities.

Even after several years, the Kok Report must be signalled for the foresight of its analysis and stands among the most relevant documents of the long-lasting and controversial debate on employment policies. The stark choices, that the crisis later required, confirmed several of the priorities then identified and revealed the mistake in postponing political choices aimed at a selective and well-planned financial support, linked to the reform of the EU budget.

A critical appraisal of the role played by the Council is not only driven by the volatility of its political majorities and the consequent uneasiness in decision-making. A more specific criticism, already mentioned above, concerns the extreme informality of the trilateral social summit (now in Article 152 TFEU), structurally disconnected from the procedures of the OMC. This formation of the Council did not offer to the social partners a

[11] See Chapter 1, Section 2.6.

powerful forum in which to be heard and had very limited influence on the making of employment policies.

To this we can add another, not negligible, weakness inherent in the letter of the Treaty. Article 263 paragraph 1 TFEU indicates that the Court of Justice reviews the legality of legislative acts 'other than recommendations and opinions'. The guidelines drawn up by the Council and addressed to Member States, for the drafting of their employment policies (Article 148.2) are not justiciable. The unsound intergovernmental connections on which these policies are grounded and the lack of sanctions displayed the urgency to find other ways to cope with the economic crisis and the devastating effects it had on employment.

2 Europe 2020: The Uncertain Role of the European Council

In order to oppose the failure of the Lisbon Strategy, the tireless drafters of employment policies found a new formula. Europe 2020 is the project conceived to favour 'smart, sustainable and inclusive growth'.[12] Proposals put forward in this document are the last ring of a long chain of initiatives that European institutions carried out, to fill the gaps in the area of active labour market policies and ensure the fight against unemployment.

The agenda set in Europe 2020 is dense of proposals, all aimed at better integration of policies and better synergies of the measures to be adopted. It intersects the enforcement of the Single Market Act, encompassing an open process of reforms proposed in the Monti Report.[13]

The Lisbon Treaty (Article 121 TFEU) specifies: 'Member States shall regard their economic policies as a matter of common concern and shall coordinate them within the Council'. It is worth recalling that Articles 121 and 126 TFEU provide the legal basis to the SGP. Article 146 paragraph 2 TFEU specifies that Member States 'shall regard promoting employment as a matter of common concern and shall coordinate their action in this respect with the Council'. Hence, initiatives on employment are intrinsically connected to comprehensive economic manoeuvres, as all austerity measures later on confirmed.

In broader terms, governance techniques reappear – and this is not unexpected – within the scheme of the European Semester, with the same

[12] Communication from the Commission, *Europe 2020. A Strategy for Smart, Sustainable and Inclusive Growth*, Brussels, 3 March 2010 COM (2010) 2020.

[13] M. Monti, *A New Strategy for the Single Market, at the Service of Europe's Economy and Society, Report to the President of the European Commission José Manuel Barroso*, 9 May 2010.

limits underlined before, namely an inadequate inclusion of stakeholders and social partners in the unfolding of decisions and deadlines. Furthermore, soft law coordination required under OMC is intertwined with the SGP, which saw the light in 1997 and evolved along the lines of legislation enacted during the crisis.

In 2014 the SGP was amended in order to strengthen surveillance mechanisms. Employment and social indicators were included in the scoreboard in view of the Alert Mechanism Report. The close interconnection of policies, generated as a reaction to the crisis, have, year after year, implied a review of the targets originally set in Europe 2020. The Commission has kept control over all such procedures.

The strategy for growth and employment, at first enshrined in Europe 2020, provided, for example, that 3 per cent of the gross domestic product (GDP) should be dedicated to the financing of research and development. 75 per cent of the active population between twenty and sixty-four years old should have a job, whereas legislative interventions in the areas of climate, energy, and emission reduction, in view of the development of renewable sources of energy, should be the cornerstones of European economic development. The school dropout rate should be reduced; the percentage of citizens with a degree increased; the number of people risking falling below the poverty line reduced drastically.

These objectives were difficult to achieve during the economic and financial crisis and have been, at least in part, set aside because of the consequences provoked, especially in countries which were worst hit by austerity measures. In 2011 both the Commission[14] and the European Council[15] came to terms with a different reality and reiterated the indications to Member States to remove the obstacles, including fiscal ones, which constrained weak individuals in unemployment traps. However, this was not enough to insinuate new energy in employment policies.

The critical review of Europe 2020 links up with the reform of the European budget for the years 2014–2020 and the new planning of European structural funds. Proposals circulating at the time looked at measures specifically directed to small and medium enterprises, particularly disadvantaged in the access to credit, or to new investments in the areas of energy saving, renewable energies or the creation of programmes

[14] Communication from the Commission, *Annual Growth Survey 2012*, Brussels, 23 November 2011 COM(2011) 815 final.

[15] Conclusions of the European Council 9 December 2011, Brussels, 25 January 2012, EUCO 139/1/11 REV 1.

to support people in long-term unemployment and young people trying to enter the labour market.

Research carried on in order to follow up the effects caused by the crisis, showed that in 2008 the 'matrix' of flexicurity measures was far away from the expectations of people affected by the loss of jobs. National strategies should have been oriented to support vulnerable workers, taking into account the main objective of job security, namely the setting up of instruments to move quickly from one job to another in order to strengthen workers' protection within the labour market.[16]

The crisis diminished the aspirational side of politics and limited the choices of national legislatures within too pragmatic and short-sighted approaches. The Economic and Social Committee (Articles 301 to 304 TFEU), a consultative EU institution representing social partners and other organised interest groups, raised a critical voice when asked to evaluate connections that should have been established between European institutions and local administrations, in view of a more efficient implementation of Europe 2020.[17]

'Smart growth', a pillar of the strategy, should have been better linked to access to funding and should have promoted social cohesion. The accent should have been put on selected interventions, favouring whenever possible research and development plans with a strong focus on local needs. The Barca Report and the Commission's proposals, which the Report inspired, were caught up in the controversial discussion leading to the reform of the EU budget 2014–2020, often slowed down by endless bureaucratic impediments.

The programme for the years 2014–2020 presented by the Commission in 2011 should have unequivocally been oriented to the concession of financing only for clearly identified priority objectives. The European Social Fund, therefore, should have prioritised the achievement of objectives identified in Europe 2020, in order to have an effective impact on national systems.[18] In the 'Compact for Growth and Jobs' adopted by the

[16] Eurofound, *Flexicurity: Perspectives and Practice* (Dublin: Foundation Findings 2010), 8 ff.

[17] Opinion of the European Economic and Social Committee on 'Regional policy contributing to smart growth in Europe 2020', Com (2010) 553 final, 2011/C318/13, 14 July 2011.

[18] European Commission, Proposal for a Regulation of the European Parliament and of the Council laying down common provisions on the European Regional Development Fund, the European Social Fund, the Cohesion Fund, the European Agricultural Fund for Rural Development and the European Maritime and Fisheries Fund covered by the Common Strategic Framework and laying down general provisions on the European Regional Development Fund, the European Social Fund and the Cohesion Fund and repealing Regulation (EC) No. 1083/2006, Brussels, 14 March 2012 COM (2011) 615 final/2.

European Council in 2012 it was confirmed that, in order to achieve the objectives set in Europe 2020, Member States should have made recourse to the European Social Fund, within the Multiannual Financial Framework. This would have facilitated the adoption of the most urgent measures, including support to youth employment through internships and vocational training just after the completion of studies and through the use of temporary hiring incentives.[19]

The complexity of policies put in motion and the need to allocate resources in a virtuous and efficient way, applying objective criteria, requires the adoption of 'composite indicators', namely of sophisticated statistical techniques to measure in detail flexicurity policies.[20] For instance, the indicator referring to 'lifelong learning' has the purpose to measure not only the participation in educational programmes but also the intensity of the activities in terms of hours and costs. The indicator concerning flexible employment contracts is not only concentrated on analysing the element of flexibility at the end of the contract but also takes into account internal flexibility and the segmentation of labour markets. The indicator on active labour market policies does not focus only on the overall costs in terms of GDP, but also examines the programmes and their implementation, evaluating the cost of each person looking for a job. The indicators should capture, in other words, the equilibrium between flexibility and security with the aim of rewarding those who achieve the predetermined objectives.

The use of statistics and related methodologies is quite frequent in the practice of OMC. With regard to social policies, indicators have the merit of offering objective parameters, on which to ground the choices of national governments, in order to make their performances comparable and facilitate their assessment by European institutions. However, with regard to soft law techniques, which by definition are an alternative to harmonisation, indicators risk being overestimated, if taken as the only instrument of measurement.

In the attempt to identify ways for a deeper evaluation of legislative policies, comparative research proposed to take into account the 'perception' of security that workers have, with regard to the chances of losing their job and seeing their salaries cut. Results of comparative analysis, based on data of the European Social Survey, revealed that the most

[19] Conclusions of the European Council, Brussels, 29 June 2012, EUCO 76/12.

[20] A. Manca, M. Governatori, and M. Mascherini, *Towards a Set of Composite Indicators on Flexicurity: A Comprehensive Approach* (Luxembourg: Publications Office of the European Union 2010), publications.Jrc.ec.europa.eu/repository/handle/111111111/13518.

relevant guarantees in workers' perceptions are in the combination of four flexicurity measures, namely lifelong learning, active labour market policies, modern systems of social protection and flexible but reliable job contracts.[21]

'Flexicurity pathways', first identified by the Commission then progressively incorporated into the Council's guidelines, were inspired by a group of experts guided by a Dutch sociologist.[22] This is probably not a mere coincidence, since both in academic research and in forward-looking legislative options the Netherlands became at the time a point of reference, when compared with other countries. In particular, attention was paid to the implementation in that country of legislative reforms mixing flexibility and security in a virtuous manner, especially in the laws of 1998 and 1999 (Allocation of Workers by Intermediates Act 1998, and Flexibility and Security Act 1999) regulating temporary agency work.

The latter, an extreme example of flexible employment contracts characterised by a continuous mobility of workers among user companies, was regulated with the intent to progressively strengthen the employment of workers with temporary agencies, following an incremental scheme of access to entitlements. This novelty received great attention in comparative research and was a source of inspiration for national legislatures.

However, an overall evaluation of flexicurity policies showed that positive outcomes of the reforms adopted by national parliaments often depended on features well beyond statistical measurement. National legislators operate within cultural constraints, which affect performances of labour markets. They have to take into account trade union traditions and the role social partners play; they must rely on the functioning of labour market institutions, which often depend on the rate of trade union membership and the coverage of collective agreements. The success of the Dutch model, shaped by the legislator at the end of the 1990s, was accomplished for the efficient combination of all these factors at that particular time.

The evaluation of employment policies can also be attempted through an analysis of litigation in courts. The success of legislative options can be looked at through the lenses of divergent and changeable interpretations offered by national judges. Furthermore, the latter rely on the very relevant

[21] W. van Oorschot and H. Chung, 'Feelings of insecurity among European workers: a multilevel analysis', *European Journal of Industrial Relations*, 21 (2015), 23–37.

[22] The Expert Group chaired by the Dutch sociologist T. Wilthagen produced the report *Flexicurity Pathways. Turning Hurdles into Stepping Stones*, Brussels June 2007, an influential document in the definition of subsequent Commission guidelines.

option to file preliminary references to the CJEU, and, in the context of domestic litigations, trigger the assessment of the exact compliance of domestic law with EU law. This channel of communication between courts can also become a signal to measure the adequacy and efficiency of the choices made by national legislators.

Procedures and acts included in the OMC are, however, excluded from the competence of the CJEU. This confirms the separation between employment policies, scattered around other non-justiciable European policies, and individual rights actionable before national courts. The justiciable option has been used within subject matters – for instance, part-time and fixed-term work – regulated through Directives, which are binding sources of law. Accordingly, there are reasons to consider that, in the varied framework of regulatory solutions proposed at EU level, secondary law builds a solid structure for the protection of individual social rights. Harmonisation contributed towards closer integration of the internal market and could still constitute, in the aftermath of the crisis, the ground on which to consolidate European social law.

3 Monitoring: The Role of the Commission

I have argued that the improvement of regulatory techniques, which should have supported employment policies, to fight unemployment and create new jobs, has not been successful. It is interesting to observe that, facing this reality, the Commission extended its own prerogatives, with the declared intention to fill the basket of information with qualitative and quantitative data and prepare the ground for correcting deficiencies.

One of these attempts is monitoring focused on industrial restructuring – a wide area including company reorganisation, closures, mergers and acquisitions, downsizing, outsourcing, relocation etc. – based on information collected at national level through contact points, using press agencies as primary sources.[23]

The expected result is the understanding of companies' strategies implying the reduction of the workforce and recourse to collective redundancies. This kind of monitoring should have allowed 'anticipating change', namely foreseeing situations of strong employment risk in order to intervene in advance, often through collective bargaining and the

[23] The European Restructuring Monitor has operated since 2002 and is run by Eurofound, a tripartite agency of the EU, www.eurofound.europa.eu.

involvement of public bodies. All subject matters related to anticipation of changes in restructuring are part of the information to be delivered to European Works Councils (EWC), elected or nominated in European companies and in groups of European companies.[24]

Monitoring of industrial restructuring convinced the Commission to present a Green Paper, in view of adopting a Directive.[25] Reflections contained in the Green Paper are extremely wide and partially interlaced with flexicurity policies.

At the beginning of 2009 national governments frequently chose to reduce working time and adopt flexible working time schemes, in order to avoid lay-offs. These solutions, adopted mainly through collective bargaining in the form of concession agreements, had the short-term effect of lowering the level of productivity and reducing salaries.

'Anticipating change' should have meant, under such circumstances, tackling work organisations and ascertaining the direction of training, with a view to creating new professional profiles, with the support of the European Social Fund. The loss of jobs should have convinced policy-makers that different paths had to be taken to diversify workers' competences, even through tailor-made programmes adaptable to groups of companies or to productive chains, both within national and transnational boundaries. A new system of incentives was supposed to stimulate domestic legislative policies, and to make recourse to the European Social Fund and other EU funds.

This programme was recapitulated in a Commission's Quality Framework – yet another soft law source, not a Directive, as first announced by the Commission – suggesting best practices in industrial restructuring.[26] The Commission had foreseen a revision of this purely

[24] Revised Directive 2009/38 EC of the European Parliament and of the Council of 6 May 2009 on the establishment of a European Works Council or a procedure in Community-scale undertakings and Community-scale groups of undertakings for the purposes of informing and consulting employees. A general framework for informing and consulting on various issues including restructuring in companies with more than fifty employees is in Directive 2002/14 EC of the European Parliament and of the Council of 11 March 2002 establishing a general framework for informing and consulting employees in the European Community – Joint declaration of the European Parliament, the Council and the Commission on employee representation.

[25] Commission Green Paper, Restructuring and anticipation of change: what lessons from recent experience, January 2012 (IP/12/23). The EP responded with a Resolution on information and consultation of workers, anticipation and management of restructuring, 15 January 2013.

[26] Communication from the Commission to the European Parliament, the Council, the European Economic and Social Committee and the Committee of the Regions, EU

voluntary method for the anticipation of change, but information and consultation of workers and their representatives disappeared from the agenda, despite the consistent number of lay-offs occurring during the crisis. The weaknesses inherent in responsible managerial choices, which are left without legal sanctions and without credible alternatives for managing the effects of the crisis, are tangible. It is noteworthy that a different route has been chosen by some large multinationals, in entering transnational framework agreements and dealing at that level with such matters.[27]

In the context of restructuring and of related finances for reskilling laid-off workers or helping them start new activities, mention must be made of the European Globalisation Adjustment Fund. It started to operate in 2007, to cope with unemployment due to major structural changes occurring in local markets, as one of the effects of globalisation. In 2009 it was then extended to include workers hit by the effects of the economic and financial crisis.[28] Financial resources provided under this scheme are activated on requests coming from Member States showing evidence of specific employment crises and are assigned on a case-by-case basis. The European Globalisation Adjustment Fund is also connected with the targets set in Europe 2020 and is supported by a budget line of its own within the multiannual financial framework 2014–2020.

In 2014, a regulation was approved for providing aid to 'persons suffering from material, or even severe material deprivation'. In 2011, one year after the launch of Europe 2020, the number of people trapped in such tragic conditions had increased, to reach nearly 8 per cent of Union citizens. This Fund is meant 'to alleviate the forms of extreme poverty with the greatest social exclusion impact, such as homelessness, child poverty and food deprivation', without interfering with national public policies. Programmes of this kind, based on co-financing, as for other EU funding, and on shared management of the Commission and Member States, should take into account cases of countries undergoing temporary budget difficulties and be kept under the Commission's close scrutiny.[29]

Quality Framework for anticipation of change and restructuring, Brussels, 13 December 2013 COM (2013) 882 final.

[27] See Chapter 3.

[28] The latest amendments are in Regulation (EU) No. 1309/2013 of the European Parliament and of the Council of 17 December 2013 on the European Globalisation Adjustment Fund (2014–2020) and repealing Regulation (EC) No. 1927/2006.

[29] Regulation (EU) No. 223/2014 of the European Parliament and of the Council of 11 March 2014 on the Fund for European Aid to the Most Deprived.

I have repeatedly underlined that European employment policies rest on non-binding rules. Monitoring on industrial restructuring, which the Commission tenaciously promoted over the years, is grounded on a voluntary method signalling best practices. Monitoring may easily develop into a technocratic method, left in the hands of experts who collect data and draft reports, but may be disconnected from national institutions. Apart from the weak impact on policy-making, this method lessens the political content of deliberative processes and, in the long term, subtracts authority from the legislative method.

To confirm this accentuated tendency towards the use of an experimental method, typical of the Europe 2020 agenda, in 2010 the Commission started monitoring trends within national labour markets, in order to provide a close analysis of data on unemployment with a view to matching new skills with new jobs. The European Vacancy Monitor highlighted demand and offer in national labour markets, to show the need for better oriented qualifications in order to escape 'bottle necks' and exploit new potentialities through well-targeted training initiatives. Data were collected from national statistic agencies, employment centres, temporary work agencies and job offers online, in the twenty-eight Member States.[30]

Cedefop, the specialised European agency responsible for vocational training, confirmed the anomaly of the employment crisis in the EU, consisting in the lack of a sufficiently qualified workforce, especially in sectors affected by technological change or by the necessity to progressively transform production processes, such as in the green economy.[31] This is a contradiction generated by the dynamics of national labour markets and by the lack of coordination at EU level. Anticipation of change has not yet been fully translated into successful practices, but the attention of EU institutions on this matter has not vanished.[32]

30 European Vacancy Reports are issued by the Commission, DG Employment and social affairs for the promotion of active labour market policies.

31 European Centre for the Development of Vocational Training (Cedefop), *Identification of Future Skill Needs for the Green Economy*, No. 2368, 2009.

32 A revised version of the European Qualification Framework has been adopted on 24 May 2017: Council Recommendation on the European Qualifications Framework for lifelong learning and repealing the Recommendation of the European Parliament and of the Council of 23 April 2008 on the establishment of the European Qualifications Framework for lifelong learning.

4 Active Labour Market Policies

In 2009 the European network of public employment services promptly reclaimed its fundamental role in the handling of new difficult times.[33] The activation of institutions to govern labour markets and enhance employment policies is often hit by the scarcity of available resources. This exacerbates inequalities in the offer of services, ineludibly showing all possible connections among social cohesion and employment policies, especially in economically disadvantaged areas.

After some years, the Council adopted a Decision addressed to Member States; a binding legal act, supported by specific resources, for the creation of a network of public employment services.[34] This very important step forward is a return to a hard law method and it is intertwined with accompanying implementing measures. In particular 'benchlearning' – it is clarified in the preamble – is an innovation meant to create links 'between benchmarking and mutual learning activities, that consists in identifying good performances through indicator-based benchmarking systems, including data collection, data validation, data consolidation and assessments, with appropriate methodology, and of using findings for tangible and evidence-informed mutual learning activities, including good or best practice models'.

Implementation of targets set in Europe 2020 is, in the words of the Decision, improved. The Commission, through a delegated act, following a formal conferral of powers for the years 2014–2020, can change the annex to the Decision, dealing with benchmarking indicators. The recourse to these sources, which has become more frequent in recent years, is such to combine the legal certainty of a binding act with the necessary changes caused by rapid innovations and new trends in labour markets. Monitoring, in this specific case, is not separated by formal outcomes connected with the implementation of the EU Decision.

Cooperation throughout the network implies the exchange of information and the adoption of related measures. The creation of best practices to favour growth and employment should end the isolation of school systems or other educational institutions and make them permeable to the real

[33] Opinion from the Public Employment Services Network to the Employment Committee, Stockholm, 3–4 December 2009.

[34] Decision No. 573/2014/EU of the European Parliament and of the Council of 15 May 2014 on enhanced cooperation between Public Employment Services. The legal basis for the Decision is Article 45 TFEU on free movement of workers and Article 46 TFEU, which should ensure cooperation among employment services.

needs of companies. Qualifications and skills should not be considered statically, as if people in search of jobs were mere containers of knowledge sporadically acquired. Qualifications should follow a dynamic educational path, continuously adaptable to the professional profiles that the market requires. Hence, the requisites of active labour market policies are those accompanying workers during their careers, providing counselling, peer-to-peer assistance and guidance to support crosscutting competences.

Along these lines, one other novelty – expressly recalled in the Decision, therefore connected to its own implementation – is the Council Recommendation launching the programme 'Youth guarantee', addressed to young people who left school and who, within four months, should be directed towards internships or vocational training. The preamble states that this is a way of 'avoiding the very high costs of having young people neither in employment, education or training (NEETs)'.[35] The Recommendation – a non-binding legal act – encompasses several options, such as supportive measures for the integration in labour markets, labour market related measures and the use of EU funds. This latter indication is of utmost importance, since it prompted recourse to funds not yet spent under the 2007–2013 programmes and the optimal preparation for funding in the years 2014–2020.

The President of the Commission, Juncker, launched another initiative addressed to young people in search of an occupation, which also aims at rebuilding trust in solidarity. The programme 'European solidarity corps', active since 7 December 2016, is open for registration to young people who want to volunteer or work in promoting social inclusion and bringing support to vulnerable people. Registration is also open for organisations, both national and international, working in these fields.[36]

Finally, having regard to Article 46 TFEU, the Council has taken yet another initiative, this time in the form of a binding regulation, which re-establishes the network of European employment services (EURES), drawing on the CJEU's case law for a broad definition of workers, fully entitled with the right to work and to move across frontiers.[37] The peculiarity of this source is to develop the coordination of the Commission with public

[35] Council Recommendation of 22 April 2013 on establishing a Youth Guarantee, 2013/C 120/01.

[36] See europa.eu/youth/solidarity_en.

[37] Regulation (EU) 2016/589 of the European Parliament and of the Council of 13 April 2016 on a European network of employment services (EURES), workers' access to mobility services and the further integration of labour markets, and amending Regulations (EU) No. 492/2011 and (EU) No. 1296/2013.

employment services and other recruitment services, including private and not-for-profit organisations, for the improvement of workers' mobility. A 'European coordination office' serves this purpose and a common information technology platform guarantees the efficiency of the system.

5 Concluding Remarks

All legislative choices made in recent years seem to go in the direction of a return to hard law, with a preference for active labour market measures supported by selective economic resources. The point to underline is the selectivity of choices related to financial support and a closer scrutiny of the concrete use made of EU resources. In the long run this option could prove to be the right one, if accompanied by the setting up of a new elite of national administrators, well trained in the enforcement of EU law and in the spending of public resources.

This is not enough to stop the uneasiness crossing Europe and dissolve the anxieties of whoever feels that confidence in the stability of labour markets is shaken. Choices made at EU level were not sufficiently reassuring in creating solid alternatives to fight unemployment and to overcome the consequences of the economic and financial crisis.

The 'fear of Europe', be it the result of prejudices or of persisting shortcomings in communication delivered by policy-makers, still needs to be fought back tenaciously through encompassing reforms.

One point cannot be ignored. The EU has expanded recourse to structural funding for employment policies and is concerned with a transparent administration of resources, bearing in mind disadvantages of less developed countries and regions.

Furthermore, the emphasis originally put on flexicurity measures, as the primary tool to promote employment, shows a change of direction towards initiatives prioritising active labour market policies. In this field, labour law has a long-lasting tradition within the EU and lends itself to interesting experimentations, because of its pluralist vocation and its tendency to acknowledge different regulatory techniques.

The examples offered in this chapter show an interesting contamination among different systems of norms. An on-going dialogue is kept alive between legislation and experimentation, mainly through monitoring and assessing the impact of the law.

In the following chapter, I shall concentrate on new experiments taking place at the periphery of national legal systems, within an emerging transnational legal order. To oppose the slowness of political decisions, collective organisations, acting in their autonomy, take the lead.

Such private transnational governments, large multinationals that are bearers of extremely diffused economic interests,[38] act as promoters of new synergies. The urgency required by deep changes taking place in global law and by a constant mobility of companies creates a *sui generis* demand for regulation, based on open, constantly changeable procedures and on adaptable schemes of action.

[38] C. Crouch, *The Strange Non-death of Neo-liberalism* (Cambridge: Polity 2011).

3

Beyond European 'Governance' Inside the Global Crisis

1 Transnational Collective Agreements in a New Pluralism of Sources

The economic and financial crisis has imposed numerous responsibilities on organisations representing workers and employers, related to the search for consensual solutions, and, at the same time, to limiting all forms of protectionist defence of national regimes of solidarity. Keeping the status quo unchanged does not facilitate the search for new developments. However, fears and uncertainties within the EU persistently undermine solidarity.

The Monti Report[1] oriented its suggestions around a closer integration of the European internal market and presented many streams of reforms, all due to eliminate barriers impeding economic recovery and, in a long-term perspective, enhance growth. However, the focus, put in the Report, on the role of the social partners was weak and rather sporadic, linked mainly to the effects of some controversial cases decided by the CJEU, in which the Court tried to balance the right to strike and the economic freedoms guaranteed in the Treaty.[2]

Recourse to strikes and to other traditional forms of collective industrial action acquires different meanings when exercised by the unions for the defence of national prerogatives, in contemplation of potentially disruptive effects caused by the transnational mobility of workers. These peculiarities of industrial action are only marginally addressed in the Report, but the connection of social rights with market efficiency is unequivocal.

The expansion of the global market, based on changing economic cycles and the emerging of new competitors takes place inexorably, while the enforcement of measures aiming at closer integration of the European internal market has been slow, despite the commitment

[1] See Chapter 2, Section 2, 4. [2] See Chapter 4.

announced by the EU institutions.[3] In the EU internal market distinct national identities converge. They developed on the history and the traditions of national social partners and consolidated around the enforcement of fundamental rights. Collective bargaining, though, with or without the support of legislation, moves beyond national borders and beyond the EU and expands transnationally. In this enlarging legal context defence of national identities should not be presented as an impediment to market efficiency, but acknowledged as an enduring value and a driving force in establishing a new transnational equilibrium.

Arguments developed in this chapter are based on the observation of new autonomous initiatives taken by large multinational companies and workers' representatives – be they EWCs or trade unions – in promoting transnational collective bargaining and the signature of agreements. The implication is that such peculiar private governments have acted quickly, seeking their own responses to the global crisis. Following a scheme of self-determination, they operated transnationally, without seeking legitimacy within national legal orders.

To describe these developments interrelated with the activism of organisations representing collective interests and to evaluate their effect on employment and working conditions, I use the concept of 'transnational juridification'.[4] I argue that the social spheres included in transnational bargaining expand the pluralism of sources governing labour relations and invent new ways of setting rules and enforcing procedures. Collective deliberations taken within transnational agreements are not binding in a strict legal sense. This is why a thought-provoking discussion has been started on how to construct a legal framework, compatible with EU law.[5]

Trade unions have been capable of reacting promptly to transnational challenges and reshaping their own internal rules.[6] In 2006 a new organisation appeared on the horizon, the 'International trade union confederation', following the merger of the dissolved 'International federation of free trade unions' and the 'World confederation of labour'. In 2007

[3] The so-called Five Presidents' Report insists on this perspective: European Commission, *Five Presidents' Report: Completing Europe's Economic and Monetary Union* (2015), available at ec.europa.eu/priorities/economic-monetary-union/docs/5-presidents-report_en.pdf.

[4] I borrow this terminology from G. Teubner (ed.), *Juridification of Social Spheres* (Berlin-New York: de Gruyter 1987).

[5] S. Sciarra, 'Resocialising collective deliberations', in N. Countouris and M. Freedland (eds.), *Resocialising Europe* (Cambridge University Press 2014), 414 ff.

[6] R. Erne, *European Unions, Labor's Quest for a Transnational Democracy* (Ithaca and London: Cornell University Press 2008), 119 ff.

so-called global unions were associated within the 'Council of global unions', with the objective of promoting collective bargaining at transnational level and spreading respect of fundamental rights. 'IndustriAll Global Union', founded in 2012, is a cross-sector organisation which brings together former global federations and is particularly active in promoting and signing transnational collective agreements.

Changes in organisations represent a reaction to changing interests at stake and aim at searching for new formulas in representing large numbers of workers. They confirm an emerging transnational dimension of industrial relations and the corresponding need to represent collectively both employers and workers, irrespective of previous and more ideological affiliations. Hence, the expansion of transnational collective agreements is not a marginal phenomenon and must be addressed in its legal contours, as well as in its practical implications.

EWCs have been involved in the anticipation of changes related to restructuring and in handling the effects of the same. The 2009 Recast Directive[7] does not explicitly empower them with bargaining rights. It clarifies both notions of information and consultation (Article 2 letters f and g) and highlights the accuracy of such notions with regard to the level of decision-making inside European companies or groups of companies whenever transnational issues are at stake (Article 1 paragraph 3). In addition, there is a more precise indication that EWC 'represent collectively the interests of the employees' (Article 10 paragraph 1).

The Recast Directive attaches more importance to 'protection and guarantees' for EWC members in the exercise of their functions, similar to those provided for employees' representatives by 'the national legislation and/or practice in force in their country of employment' (Article 10 paragraph 3).

However, there is no lack of critical voices with regard to collective representation, since this too-generic formula does not expressly extend to the legal capacity to appear before a court. Furthermore, traditional

[7] Directive 2009/38/EC of the European Parliament and of the Council of 6 May 2009 on the establishment of a European Works Council or a procedure in Community-scale undertakings and Community-scale groups of undertakings for the purposes of informing and consulting employees (Recast). See F. Dorssemont and T. Blanke (eds.), *The Recast of the European Works Council Directive* (Antwerp: Intersentia 2010); A. Alaimo, 'The new Directive on European Works Councils: innovations and omissions', *International Journal of Comparative Labour Law and Industrial Relations*, 26 (2010), 217.

sanctions seem unfitted for the protection of rights activated at transnational level.[8]

The Directive on EWC, which applies to the European Economic Area (EEA) and is accordingly binding in thirty countries, manifested its potentials in many directions, allowing a diffused practice of transnational bargaining, especially on industrial restructuring. Even if not included among the objectives of the Directive, negotiations on these matters slowly developed into multiple bargaining fronts and were opened to representatives of workers employed in companies outside the EU or the EMU. The EWCs, accordingly, were named 'Global Works Councils' and contributed to redefining criteria of representation allowing, for instance, workers occupied in non-EU companies to elect representatives without the right to vote, but with a consultative role.[9]

On the expansive force of the Directive, beyond its formal scope, large multinational groups based their efforts to improve their corporate culture and moved towards the unilateral adoption of codes of conduct. This choice, facilitated by the appearance on the scene of new global trade unions, opened up new opportunities and new alliances at the bargaining table.[10]

Research carried out on such new experiments reveals that the prevalent theme of the agreements in question concerned the enforcement of fundamental rights – freedom of association and ILO core labour standards – expanded to cover transnational supply chains, characterised by economically dependent subsidiaries or sub-contractors. In addition, international framework agreements included a larger number of issues, if compared with unilateral codes of conduct. They also developed an increasing interest for harmonised levels of protection, for instance with regard to health and safety at the place of work. The monitoring system of the agreed standards is still fragile, especially in supply chains where large multinational companies take the lead in negotiations.[11]

[8] European Commission, *Implementation of Recast Directive 2009/38/EC on European Works Councils*, Report of the group of experts, December 2010.

[9] Early examples are the agreements signed in 2010 by the Donnelley group, with the headquarters based in Chicago, present in more than forty countries, including the United Kingdom in the EU, and in 2009 by the Norwegian multinational company DNV, with representatives elected in Asian, American and African companies following a criterion of proportionality calculated on the total workforce.

[10] A. Sobczak, 'Codes of conduct in subcontracting networks. a labour law perspective', *Journal of Business Ethics*, 44 (2003), 225 ff.

[11] I. Schömann, A. Sobczak, E. Voss, and P. Wilke, *Codes of conduct and international framework agreements: New forms of governance at company level* (Luxembourg: Eurofound 2008), 30 ff.; K. Papadakis (ed.), *Cross-Border Social Dialogue and Agreements:*

Experts in human relations and in company behaviour observe these new experiments and acknowledge that global unions as external actors display a more accentuated ability to modify 'managerial practices' even when enforcement mechanisms remain weak. Global unions intend to conquer the scene of collective bargaining and to do so proposing themselves as unique interlocutors in the dialogue with large multinationals, offering a more stable and resilient bargaining platform through the formalisation of bilateral binding agreements.[12]

The International Metalworkers Federation has been among the most active unions in promoting transnational bargaining. In an 'action plan' drawn for the years 2009–2013 the International Metalworkers Federation addressed to national members binding guidelines on the signature of agreements and on subsequent implementation of the same in all companies of the multinational group. This is a concrete attempt to coordinate membership at an international level with a view to enforcing transnational agreements at a national level. Following this model, several European federations have adopted internal bylaws introducing procedures for negotiations with transnational companies.[13]

This point is of utmost importance and has been highlighted in academic research and in experts' reports promoted by ETUC with the support of the European Commission. Disclosure of a clear mandate is, in fact, a way for ascertaining that national unions associated with transnational organisations become actively involved in bargaining procedures.

1.1 *Some Examples of Transnational Collective Agreements*

Among early and most innovative transnational agreements, inspired by the EWC Directive, two should be highlighted, both signed in 2010 by the multinational group GDF Suez, which operates in the energy sector.

The first one dealing with health and safety applied to companies controlled by GDF, with a participation ranging between 10 per cent

An emerging Global Industrial Relations Framework? (Geneva: International Institute for Labour Studies/International Labour Organisation 2008).

12 M. Fichter, M. Helfen, and J. Sydow, 'Employment relations in global production networks: initiating transfer of practices via union involvement', *Human Relations*, 64 (2011), 599 ff.

13 Among others, IndustriAll, EMF, EMCEF, EPSU and TLC-ETUF.

and 50 per cent. This criterion was adopted to indicate how the head-quarter exercises control over subsidiaries and how this implies their inclusion within the scope of the agreement.

The second one is a group agreement dealing with an 'employment and expertise plan', providing a proactive management of the workforce, in order to anticipate demands for new skills and favour labour mobility within the group. The agreement delves into specific measures to be implemented in order to support workers during the transition between jobs, for example with exploratory trips to the new place of work, travel allowances and mobility allowances.

A similar solution is envisaged in the Alstom agreement, signed in Paris by the European Federation of Metalworkers in 2011, dealing once more with anticipation of changes. This agreement offers solutions to internal restructuring providing for internal mobility, retraining aids, transitions to part-time jobs, allowances to start self-employed jobs or to look for a new job within the group or in other companies within the same geographical area. The agreement goes as far as exploring tailor-made measures to support workers, offering the opportunity for individual meetings with management and providing mentoring in order to identify the specific professional potential of each individual. In addition, indicators are agreed – training hours, number of tutors, number of individual meetings – useful to ensure the monitoring of mutual obligations.

The European Trade Union Federation Textiles and the EWC signed in December 2010 the Agreement DB Apparel, aimed once more to anticipate change. It provides, among other measures, that twice each year, a meeting of a task force should take place, to manage strategically a databank of professions and jobs within the group. Similar solutions within the group are foreseen for outplacement support or the development of new professional career tracks.

There are numerous agreements which concentrate on respect for fundamental rights and on ethically sensitive behaviours in large corporate groups. Again, in the GDF Suez group with regard to a global agreement on the enforcement of fundamental rights, social dialogue and sustainable development, signed in November 2010, following consultation with the company, the EWC expressed a negative opinion on the financial participation of a Chinese sovereign fund, showing serious concerns about lack of guarantees in that country in terms of corporate social responsibility and respect for human rights.

There is no lack of similar examples in the automotive sector.[14] Daimler-Chrysler – as it was named at the time of a merger in 1998 – signed one of the first global agreements with EWC, in which representation of Brazilian and South African workers was foreseen. This multinational corporation extended to sub-contractors the obligation to respect trade union rights guaranteed by international labour law sources, to be considered part of the transnational agreements signed by workers' representatives, and went as far as contemplating the termination of contracts with companies not complying with the undertaken obligations.

More recent agreements are worth mentioning, since they address contemporary unsolved issues. Safran, a company operating in aerospace and defence security, and IndustriAll signed an agreement in 2015, following the enforcement of a 2013 agreement for the professional integration of young people. The company stipulates skills and career paths for group's employees throughout Europe, whereby managers are made responsible for the assessment of individual skills and the identification of training facilities and professional mobility. Best practices are quoted in the text of the agreement, to show ways for measuring the efficiency of the training received.

In 2015 Total and IndustriAll signed a global agreement on corporate social responsibility for the promotion of human rights at the workplace. Relevant points in this text are the relations that the group establishes with contractors and suppliers, in order to bind them to the observation of specific clauses in the agreement, making sure to communicate and promote them appropriately. If the agreement is not enforced, the group 'will take the necessary action, which may go as far as terminating the contract' (Articles 2–5). Furthermore, the group operates 'the selection of its contractors and suppliers on the basis of their ability to comply with its policy on safety, health, environment and quality'. If there is no compliance, the sanction is, in this case too, as serious as terminating the contract (Articles 4–5).

Looking at novelties emerging at transnational level, one cannot disregard the weaknesses that a new transnational system of industrial

[14] I. Da Costa and U. Rehfeldt, 'Transnational restructuring agreements. General overview and specific evidence from the European Automobile Sector', in K. Papadakis (ed.), *Shaping Global Industrial Relations. The Impact of International Framework Agreements* (Geneva: ILO Palgrave Macmillan 2011), 143 ff.; I. Da Costa and U. Rehfeldt, 'Transnational company agreements on restructuring at EU level', in S. Leonardi (ed.), *Transnational Company Agreements* (Rome: Ediesse 2012), 85 ff.

relations displays, despite the important commitments made by large corporations, with regard to ethical as well as legal issues.

The most recurring formulas adopted by the parties mainly describe strategic and organisational options of large multinational groups. It is problematic to attach to them a normative function, reflected on binding obligations taken by the parties who sign the agreement. It is equally difficult to follow an interpretation similar to the one adopted for national collective agreements and argue that workers employed in companies covered by transnational agreements acquire enforceable rights, for instance to the stability of their jobs, should there be a failure to enact procedures for labour mobility within the multinational or should measures for professional requalification and new training opportunities not come into effect.

In a similar vein to what Europe 2020 pictures in some of its proposals, particularly the ones related to anticipation of changes in matching skills and professional profiles with companies' demands, transnational agreements propose a mix of ethics and efficiency. The safeguarding of jobs whenever companies undergo restructuring is explained in terms of new opportunities for training and education within the multinational group. All such open processes are presented as parallel routes to active labour market policies, which should have been the result of national reforms. Lifelong learning, a leading component of flexicurity policies, should be a most significant part of states' obligations and is, at the same time, an opportunity for workers covered by transnational agreements.

Professional career tracks, identified by the signatories of the agreements mentioned above, aim at building consensus within large private governments, detecting working opportunities and improvements in the acquisition of skills. These chances, made available for workers, in no way resemble traditional individual rights; neither do they provide individual entitlements in a strict legal sense. They follow a different pattern, which implies support to individual expectations and develops along the lines of merely procedural obligations.

The outcomes of transnational collective agreements display new dimensions of solidarity, essentially constructed on social consensus within large multinationals. This scheme can be interpreted as an alternative to social conflict, at least to traditional industrial actions aimed at obtaining better working conditions and increased wages. It is, in fact, worth noting that wage bargaining falls outside the scope of transnational agreements, whereas it remains within the competences of national collective bargaining.

This latter point should not be underestimated. Research promoted by the ILO, covering the years mostly affected by the crisis, demonstrates that wage policies carried out at national level through collective bargaining contribute to lowering social inequality, enhancing, at the same time, economic growth and productivity-related wage increases, assuring, among other things, the elasticity of salary fluctuations. In countries where collective agreements are binding and cover wide sectors of productive activities, less inequality in wage levels is reported.

These data confirm the re-equilibrating function played by private governments, whenever large and stable organisations representing workers and employers operate.[15] However, wage growth stagnated in 2014–2015 and inequalities grew, also as a direct consequence of poor growth in wages.[16] The impulse that can be given by national governments and legislatures cannot be underestimated whenever private actors prove too weak in the effort to promote wage increases. National collective bargaining, supported when necessary by legislation, should by all means continue to be the driving force in setting wage standards, a purpose not pre-empted by transnational bargaining.

Many critical issues emerge from the analysis of transnational collective agreements. Neither can such agreements be assimilated to national collective agreements – be they national or local or decentralised at company level – nor should replicate these formats. They should occupy a place of their own in the multilevel structure of collective bargaining. This is, after all, the novelty brought about by the globalisation of markets and of the economic actors.

Another critical point to be addressed is whether transnational agreements, because of their peculiar latitude, may end up having a more limited scope with regard to the subject matters included in negotiations, and be essentially restricted only to issues related to the transnational mobility of workers and companies.

Should such a more limited scope be envisaged, transnational negotiators could find that outstanding economic and political goals, such as fighting wage dumping and enforcing the fundamental

[15] ILO, *Global Wage Report 2008/2009*, 41–3, www.ilo.org/wcmsp5/groups/public/—dgreports/—dcomm/documents/publication/wcms_100786.pdf.

[16] ILO, *Global Wage Report 2014/2015*, www.ilo.org/wcmsp5/groups/public/—dgreports/—dcomm/—publ/documents/publication/wcms_324678.pdf.

principle of equal treatment among workers affected by the mobility of companies and workers of the host country where they move to, should not be taken on board and rather be left to legislatures and policy-makers.

Transnational agreements are indeed promoted by large companies and become pivotal to their economic strategies. There are good reasons to argue that they should comply with the law of the countries in which both headquarters of multinationals and all connected branches operate. Hence, states should be active in monitoring that no infringements of fundamental rights occur. Private governments must occupy their own places within legal systems and display autonomy of their choices, without contrasting the law.

The newest element – and for this reason the most controversial one – is the identification of collective negotiators' legitimacy in bargaining at transnational level. This concerns their participation in negotiations and the identification of a clear mandate that can safely lead to the signature of agreements. The latter do not modify existing national levels of collective agreements, nor do they interfere with their enforcement. Enhancing legal certainty becomes a far more complex aftermath in transnational negotiations, which are not assisted by industrial action, or by alternative dispute resolutions. Consequently, the emphasis must be placed on strengthening the mandate of transnational negotiators.[17]

The terminology adopted so far is a symptom of the many implications hidden in these new bargaining procedures. 'European transnational agreements' are allegedly limited to companies operating within the EU, whereas 'international framework agreements' or 'global agreements' expand beyond the boundaries of the EU. There are cases, however, in which European agreements include in the negotiations observers representing workers employed in subsidiaries located outside the EU.

These 'texts', as the European Commission defines them,[18] are not easily framed within traditional schemes. It is of utmost importance that in 2013 the Commission chose to store them in a dedicated archive.[19] The Commission's purpose is to promote social dialogue, in line with the

[17] A. Lo Faro, 'Bargaining in the shadow of "optional frameworks"? The rise of transnational collective agreements and EU law', *European Journal of Industrial Relations*, 18 (2012), 11.

[18] Staff Working Document of 2008 on the Role of Transnational Collective Agreements (SEC (2008) 2155).

[19] The European Commission, DG Employment, Social Affairs and Inclusion set up a database: ec.europa.eu/social/main.jsp?catId=978. The texts available are both European and global framework agreements.

Treaty (Articles 152 and 153 TFEU) and to further enhance fundamental rights (Articles 27 and 28 EU Charter of Fundamental Rights). The bond with Europe 2020 should easily be established, since transnational texts are apt to solve broad operations of restructuring within large companies, taking into account specific solutions for each company.[20]

1.2 An Optional Legal Framework for Transnational Agreements

The Commission's commitment in supporting transnational bargaining is proved by the promotion of research and by support offered to several expert groups. ETUC, in particular, concentrated its efforts in the search for solutions which can guarantee legal certainty. Two recent reports, drawn by independent academics, tackle the issues which are most relevant in the context of this chapter and have emerged from the description of transnational agreements.[21]

It is noteworthy that ETUC has formally taken the position to provide a legal basis for transnational bargaining (Article 6 TEU, Articles 152, 154 and 156 TFEU) and suggest the adoption of an optional legal framework, namely a Decision of the Council and of the European Parliament (Article 288 TFEU) or a Decision of the social partners (Article 155 TFEU).

Decisions are legal acts of the EU, which, if there is no indication of specific addressees, are binding in their entirety and are addressed to Member States. They are often accompanied by delegated acts of the Commission, empowered by the same Decisions to adopt non-legislative acts 'to supplement or amend certain non-essential elements of the legislative acts' (Article 290 TFEU). Decisions adopted by the social partners reflect the spirit of social dialogue, enshrined in the Treaty. More specifically, they encompass the process of autonomous contractual relations,

[20] See also the motion for a European Parliament resolution on cross-border collective bargaining and transnational social dialogue, presented by the Committee on employment and social affairs (rapporteur: Thomas Händel) in June 2013 (pe508.017v02-00), followed by European Parliament resolution of 12 September 2013 on cross-border collective bargaining and transnational social dialogue (2012/2292(INI)).

[21] ETUC, *Towards a Legal Framework for Transnational Agreements, Report to the European Trade Union Confederation*, Group of experts: S. Sciarra, M. Fuchs, and A. Sobczak (Brussels 2014). At the time of writing this publication, the present writer was not yet a sitting judge in the Constitutional Court. See also *Building an Enabling Environment for Voluntary and Autonomous Negotiations at Transnational Level between Trade Unions and Multinational Companies* (Brussels 2016). This latter project was carried out by ETUC in partnership with EPSU, ETF, IndustriAll and UNI Europa.

including agreements, concluded at Union level, which can be implemented by a Council decision on a proposal from the Commission (Article 155.2 TFEU).

The most provocative part of the proposal lies in the combination of 'optional' and 'legal' as joint elements of the framework. The intention is not to interfere with autonomous self-determination of transnational negotiators – this is the 'option' left for them – and, at the same time, build up a legally relevant scheme of mutual obligations. If no option is taken in order to enter the legal framework, transnational agreements continue to fluctuate in the current soft law environment, in which bona fide obligations mainly rest in the powerful hands of multinational companies, free to enforce them throughout the chain of subsidiaries. It is worth noting that companies have so far acted without the support of European employers' associations and in fact disregard their critical view on the matter.

ETUC favours the adoption of a legal framework and goes as far as drafting in detail the proposal for a Decision. This should not be surprising in the light of what I have described before, namely an accentuated role of European and global trade unions in seeking to acquire a formal mandate for transnational negotiations, in order to represent their membership and guarantee the enforcement of the agreements at national level, where companies of the multinational group are located.

This widespread and growing activism shows a clear-cut demarcation with the role that should be assigned to EWCs. The latter are not formally excluded from the joint signature of transnational agreements, but accepted in recognition of a consolidated corporate culture.[22] The latest ETUC proposal is very cautious on this point and clarifies that the Decision establishing the optional legal framework should not expand the competence of EWCs.

At the other side of the bargaining table, the headquarters of large companies have to acquire consent throughout the multinational group. Legal enforceability of the agreements may become the emblem of solid industrial relations and accomplish the goal of uniform compliance of contractual obligations. ETUC's proposal indicates that, once it is ascertained that the company is transnational, disclosure of the mandate should

[22] I. Schömann et al., *Transnational Collective Bargaining At Company Level. A New Component of European Industrial Relations* (Brussels: ETUI 2012); M. Cilento, 'Development of transnational negotiations with multinational companies in a trade union perspective', in Leonardi (ed.) *Transnational Company Agreements*, supra n. 14, 180 ff.

consist in expressly mentioning the subsidiaries covered by the negotiations and how the same are bound by the agreement.

Transnational agreements signed in the aftermath of the crisis, in anticipation of changes caused by restructuring may, as a consequence, marginalise conflict and favour new consensual regimes of solidarities among workers. However, the optional legal framework endorsed by ETUC clarifies that fundamental rights – including the right to strike – guaranteed by national legal systems, should not be put under threat. Precedence should be given to solving disputes, if necessary referring to a mediating body designated for this purpose and exercising the right to strike as *extrema ratio*. This is one of the subject matters that should appropriately be delegated to the Commission (Article 290 TFEU), following the indications of Article 154 TFEU. This latter article entrusts the Commission with initiatives aimed at encouraging all forms of dialogue between labour and management.

The step taken by ETUC in opening up to alternative dispute resolution is innovative and demonstrates the attention paid by this large organisation representing European workers to the expectations of companies engaged in such complex bargaining procedures. Delegation of powers to the Commission is foreseen and could prove particularly useful in facilitating the adaptation of the relevant clauses to different national legal cultures and ensuring the efficient enforceability of the same. The panel should be composed of mediators appointed by each signatory party, leaving to the Commission the appointment of the third independent member.

The Commission should also be in charge of collecting the agreements, making them publically accessible and noting all changes occurring in the composition of the bargaining agents, for example in the number of subsidiaries within the multinational company. This point, too, is part of the proposal and confirms the intention to formalise bargaining procedures, with a close involvement of the Commission.

One final point to mention is that transnational agreements should include a non-regression clause, namely the obligation not to prejudice or reduce the general level of protection afforded to workers at national level, whereas most favourable conditions provided by transnational agreements should always prevail.

This brief summary of proposals put forward by ETUC with regard to an optional legal framework grounded in the Treaty and meticulously tailored around the practice of transnational negotiations developed so far, is relevant for the argument I presented in the opening lines of this chapter.

Collective deliberations at transnational level show the liveliness of autonomous private governments and a rising pluralism of sources in the regulation of labour relations, in the aftermath of the economic and financial crisis. Solidarity is seeking new aggregations and new ways of reaching those who are most in need of representation. Conflict, too, is adapting to different industrial relations and to changing circumstances, due mainly to the opening up of global markets and to the mobility of companies therein.

2 'Transnational Juridification'

In the section above I have offered a few examples of transnational collective agreements, which confirm the rising activism of private organisations representing collective interests during the crisis and possibly despite of it. Transnational bargaining takes place in a vacuum of detailed legal provisions. However, strong legal underpinnings are, on the one hand, freedom of association and, on the other, the Lisbon Treaty, which promotes the social partners at the Union level 'taking into account the diversity of national systems', as well as facilitating their dialogue and respecting their autonomy. The Charter of Fundamental Rights guarantees to 'workers and employers, or their respective organisations' the right of collective bargaining (Article 28).

I have also highlighted some relevant and recurring contents of the agreements, which take on board the anticipation of changes in company restructuring and other measures, such as workers' mobility and the matching of new skills with new jobs, which are also included in the Europe 2020 agenda. These texts are not purely declamatory. They tackle the effects of company strategies and try to compensate for the delays of political decision-making. This is why growing interest in institutional discussions is devoted to searching for legal formulas which can better structure the scheme of mutual obligations agreed by the parties and make them durable, with a view, whenever necessary, to out-of-court dispute resolution.

Having this in mind as a background, it is urgent to identify the origin of normative powers exercised by transnational bargaining agents, going beyond national competences and beyond states as regulators. The issue at stake – not only a theoretical one, as it clearly emerges looking at developments in the scope of transnational agreements – has to do with the role played by states. The latter should be the ones to empower private organisations – non-governmental organisations, interest groups, trade unions and organisations representing employers – in view of identifying transnational collective interests and connecting them to national legal systems. They should also be the guarantors of respect for fundamental rights and for fair working conditions.

Political scientists have been debating different perspectives on 'the end of states', some of them placing excessive emphasis on governance and the amplification of roles that private entities have occupied. The case of transnational collective bargaining proves the dependency of private parties on state support and the urgency to reconsider that legitimacy in processes of norm setting should emanate from state authority.

Progresses in transnational bargaining are good examples to strengthen the theory of states as managers and coordinators of denationalised entities and to contradict incomplete theories on governance.[23] Moreover, these progresses show that democratic principles must constantly accompany the expansion of private governments and complement the integration of the market. Transnational bargaining, as already mentioned, articulates fundamental rights, enshrined in national constitutional traditions and in EU primary law. In such a way it could become beneficial to better integration.

A similar concern on theories intending to go beyond the state is shared in historical investigation. The search for the origin of normative powers should not be taken away from nation-states. The suggested notion of 'constitutional legitimacy' explains how constitutional principles have created a delegated agency relationship among Member States and EU supranational institutions. Constitutional bodies of the Member States, which are deeply embedded in national institutional history, act as the principals in the integration process and the EU institutions ultimately should serve as agents. National administration should, in the end, continue to be the ones who better influence EU institutions and fulfil the objective of closer integration.[24]

This representation of historical developments within the EU clarifies, at least in part, current dissatisfaction with institutional choices departing from a traditional European legal method and opting for

[23] *Ex multis*, P. Genschel and B. Zangl, 'Transformations of the State: From Monopolist to Manager of Political Authority', Transtate Working Papers, 76/2008.

[24] P. Lindseth, *Power and Legitimacy: Reconciling Europe and the Nation-State* (Oxford, Oxford University Press, 2010).

intergovernmental deliberations. It also confirms that the authority arising from state administrations is constitutionally sound and complements the deficiencies of an incomplete project of political integration of the EU.

Between the end of the 1990s and the beginning of the year 2000, the emphasis given to soft law and to non-binding procedures, especially in the management of employment policies within the EU, contributed to weaken the authority of regulatory states. Governance techniques developed in those years did not, however, prevent collective organisations representing employers and workers to conquer and express new normative powers.

The experimental method proposed within the OMC should have been based on an exchange of good practices among state administrations and Member States bureaucratic elites, coordinated by the Commission, which was responsible towards the Council in the context of non-binding procedures.[25] The prevalence of a clearly technocratic attitude in the management of employment and social inclusion policies is, accordingly, an unexpected outcome of the functioning of European governance, as initially defined by the Commission.

Backed by the support of influential academic research,[26] which was oriented to expanding the role of civil society in decision-making processes, the Commission favoured at the time the fluidity of deliberative processes. The result was the weakening of the OMC and the dispersion of the political function of coordination, institutionally earmarked to the Council.

Procedural methods, on which governance is mainly based, have become, with the passing of time, instruments of communication rather than unambiguous regulatory techniques. Governance should, instead, tend to favour a mix of roles between public and private actors and strengthen the pluralism of sources. I have pointed to ways in which transnational collective agreements go into the direction of providing articulate and adaptable systems of norms that can easily be connected to

[25] C. Barnard, 'The shaky legal foundations for institutional action under the Employment, Lisbon and EU 2020 Strategies' in C. Barnard and O. Odudu (eds.), *Cambridge Yearbook of European Legal Studies 2009–2010*, XII (Oxford: Hart Publishing 2010), 16.

[26] J. Zeitlin, 'Social Europe and experimentalist governance: towards a new constitutional compromise?', in G. de Búrca (ed.), *EU Law and the Welfare State: In Search of Solidarity* (Oxford University Press 2005). See also, among the many research projects promoted by the Commission, C. Joerges and O. Gerstenberg (eds.), *Private Governance, Democratic Constitutionalism and Supranationalism* (Luxembourg: European Commission 1998).

national systems of collective bargaining. Although one should not overestimate the functions and the expectations assigned to these agreements and be aware that figures, so far, only cover a limited number of workers throughout the EU, it is still useful to reflect on this novelty and build on it for the future.

The attempts to fasten these agreements to a legal framework and to accentuate the element of legal certainty as an expected outcome of transnational negotiations are the most recent steps taken towards a new feature of what I suggest calling 'transnational juridification'. My suggestion is inspired by scholarship developed towards the end of the 1980s, which explored the social spheres where law is created through the active role played by different actors embedded in civil society.[27] In that narrative, pluralism of sources is connected to pluralism of actors, capable of generating applicable standards and enforcing them within the social spheres.

The social spheres to be observed are today numerous and more complex, because they are in communication with a legal order losing connection with a well-defined territory and changing the definition of its normative borders. Constitutional theories should aim to confer legitimacy on the entities representing collective interests while interpreting and assimilating transnational sources.

In this on-going course the regulation of the market does not acquire a moral connotation of its own, detached from the guarantee of democratic principles. The proliferation of social spheres, including the ones examined in this chapter, confirms the vitality of law-making at the periphery of states, without losing contact with states' authority. In critical phases for the evolution of welfare states, when the scarcity of resources imposes the adoption of fair redistributive criteria, it is vital to attach the aim of market integration to constitutional principles.

'Transnational juridification' of social spheres – as I suggest naming this phenomenon – should provide a theoretical framework and include collective bargaining in its constantly evolving features. The latter is a persuasive source of innovation at the transnational level and an opportunity for the EU in the aftermath of the crisis.

The open and continuous process of integration, which has been described as 'ordering' rather than 'ordered' pluralism, acknowledges the 'indeterminacy, inconsistency and instability accompanying the internationalisation of law'. This is due, among other reasons, to the

[27] G. Teubner (ed.), *Juridification of Social Spheres* (Berlin-New York, De Gruyter 1987).

proliferation of international bodies and private organisations. Interactions among different legal systems become normative, since they deal with the 'ought to be' rather than the 'is'. A flexible hierarchy of sources is the final result of such interactions, which should favour coordination and judicial dialogue.[28]

The description I offered, taking the example of transnational collective agreements, adds yet another dimension to 'ordering pluralism'. The connection I made with the critique of governance, clarifies the urgency to search for clear legitimacy of the actors who bear the responsibility in setting normative patterns. Flexible interactions among multiple sources should not impede the determination of principles enhancing legal certainty. Judicial dialogue can only grow on the interpretation of clear legal principles. These are the reasons why juridification of transnational practices leading to the signature of legally relevant texts should be framed within a forward-looking process of integration.

The current critical state of European integration shows the need to return to states as sources of constitutional democracy. My suggestion is that European social and employment policies constitute the ground on which to test the best ways to make such a return possible and concrete.

2.1 Solidarity, 'Social Dumping', Productive Chains: The Quest for Fundamental Rights

The mobility of companies and workers can add uncertainties to the destabilising effects of the crisis, whenever it fosters differentiation in regimes of solidarity. This happens when companies choose to exploit in a competitive way the lower cost of labour through social dumping. This practice, which was unknown in the early days of the EEC, has become part of a public discussion following some controversial decisions of the CJEU. In the cases from which that litigation originated and became the content of preliminary ruling procedures filed with the CJEU, solidarity regimes were in collision and no mechanism was in place to compensate for differences in treatment, except recourse to conflict and in particular to the right to strike.[29]

[28] M. Delmas-Marty, *Ordering Pluralism: A Conceptual Framework for Understanding the Transnational Legal World* (Oxford: Hart Publishing 2009), 14–15.

[29] See Chapter 4.

On the contrary, there should be ways to show that social dumping can profitably be corrected, avoiding the adoption of competitive regimes for wages and working conditions. An example is provided in Norway, where a governmental plan was adopted in order to fight social dumping, which is frequent in the construction sector, where temporary work agencies post workers across borders. The plan provides for equal wages and working conditions for foreign and Norwegian workers. Respect of such standards is enforced by national authorities – the Labour Inspection Authority and the Petroleum Safety Authority Norway – which also have the power to inspect companies. Norway also created a register dedicated to listing temporary work agencies operating in Norway, with the objective of controlling elusive practices of the legislation in force.[30]

In Denmark, since March 2011, we encounter an anti-dumping agreement, signed by the large workers federation 3F and by the organisations representing small and medium enterprises in the construction sector. The agreement provides for the obligation to enter contracts only with companies applying collective agreements, an obligation which can be enforced through litigation in court. Moreover, a special fund was introduced, in which a percentage of the hourly wage is collected with the aim of developing forms of cooperation in the fight against social dumping. This first attempt should stimulate more extensive agreements aiming to introduce shared responsibility in productive chains.[31]

In Finland, the posting of workers through chains of contractors and sub-contractors particularly touches construction and shipbuilding sectors, where the fragmentation of the labour market caused by wage competition and differences among normative regimes is more visible. The challenge for Finnish trade unions is to prevent the lessening of attention towards their own members, who fear the loss of an established system of social protection and, at the same time, establish solidarity regimes for workers coming from weaker economies.[32]

30 *Recruiting Immigrant Workers: Norway 2014*, OECD Publishing, November 2014, dx.doi.org/10.1787/9789264226135-en. See also A. M. Ødegård, Ø. Berge, and K. Alsos, *New Regulations for Temporary Work Agencies: Can Growing Informal Market Be Subdued? A Case Study of the Norwegian Construction Sector*, a paper shown to the Congress of International Industrial Relations Association (IIRA), Copenhagen, 28 June–1 July 2010, faos.ku.dk/pdf/iirakongres2010/track1/86.pdf.

31 K. Pedersen, 'New agreement to combat social dumping', *Eurofound online*, 10 June 2011, www.Eurofound.europa.eu/eiro/2011/03/articles/dk1103019i.htm.

32 N. Lillie, 'Subcontracting, posted migrants and labour market segmentation in Finland', *British Journal of Industrial Relations*, 50 (2012), 148–67.

A preliminary reference to the CJEU, lodged by a Finnish court, dealt with the posting of Polish workers to Finland. The Court ruled in favour of equal pay for posted workers and described in great detail the structure of salaries in the building sector.[33]

The clearest contradiction emerging from the examples quoted above is the clash among solidarity regimes, in particular when a clear definition of temporary transnational posting of workers is missing and the length of the posting becomes unforeseeable.

The Monti Report was conscious of these issues and indicated that posting of workers may hide unfair practices, whenever the service provider is not economically reliable. This, too, becomes an impediment to the integration of the market, as well as an infringement of fundamental rights.[34]

The 2014 Enforcement Directive had precisely the objective to combat frauds and abuses, which were monitored under the previous 1996 Directive and were mainly caused by economically unstable entities – the so-called 'letter-box companies' – active in the posting of workers.[35] The next Proposal put forward by the Commission in 2016[36] covered issues related to social dumping and provided that mandatory rules and wages defined in collective agreements should bind cross-border service providers, in order to guarantee the principle of equal treatment for posted workers. It also dealt with the controversial notion of temporary provision of services, suggesting that whenever the posting of workers lasted for more than twenty-four months, Member States should apply national labour law and enforce the duty to disclose all elements of wages paid to posted workers. French President Macron placed this reform of EU legislation high on the list of

[33] Case C-396/13 *Sähköalojen ammattiliitto ry* v. *Elektrobudowa Spółka Akcyjna* [2015].

[34] Monti Report, 75.

[35] Directive 2014/67/EU of the Parliament and of the Council 15 May 2014 on the enforcement of Directive 96/71/EC concerning the posting of workers in the framework of the provision of services and amending Regulation (EU) No. 1024/2012 on administrative cooperation through the Internal Market Information System ('the IMI Regulation').

[36] Proposal for a Directive of the European Parliament and of the Council amending Directive 96/71/EC of the European Parliament and of the Council of 16 December 1996 concerning the posting of workers in the framework of the provision of services, 8 March 2016 COM(2016) 128 final 2016/0070 (COD). See also the Communication from the Commission to the European Parliament, the Council and the National Parliaments on the proposal for a Directive amending the Posting of Workers Directive, with regard to the principle of subsidiarity, in accordance with Protocol No. 2, 20 July 2016 COM (2016) 505 final, which addresses criticism raised by some Member States.

priorities and suggested that posting to the host country should not be longer than twelve months, thus once more postponing the final decision.[37] The relevance of the matter is such that the President of the Commission, in his 'State of the Union' address has acknowledged the urgency to intervene in setting equal wages for posted workers and has chosen to echo his call for action in an institutional forum.[38]

It is not surprising that the Proposal received the support of the EU social partners in the construction industry, together with other organisations, such as the European Builders Confederation, the European Federation of Building and Woodworkers, the Dutch Trade Union Confederation, the Estonian Trade Union Confederation and the Council of Nordic Trade Unions. This is a sector of activities traditionally affected by cross-border mobility of workers.

Over the years, despite the growing relevance of this phenomenon, it proved difficult to collect specific data on numbers of mobile workers and on the length of posting. Eurociett, the European organisation representing temporary work agencies, and the global union Uni Europa responded to such a lack of reliable information with the creation of an Observatory to monitor transnational activities of agencies. It must be mentioned that the European sector agreement, on which the observatory is based, has been for the European Commission a privileged channel to gather information and good practices. On 3 December 2009 the social partners, within the sector social dialogue signed an agreement establishing the Observatory.[39] The latter has also become a reliable source of information for the European Commission. The acknowledgment to social partners should be that collective bargaining, even in this case, provides the best instrument for correcting the deficiencies of national administrations, responsible, in the first place, for the coordination of transnational mobility of workers.

This lack of information has been, at least in part, amended by research on portable documents A1, namely the formal statements indicating the social security legislation applicable to posted workers. The Report shows how difficult it is to compare data in this field and how varied the numbers

37 See www.euractiv.com/section/economy-jobs/news/macrons-proposals-wreak-havoc-on-posted-worker-negotiations/.

38 J.-C. Juncker, 'State of the Union Address', 13 September 2017, europa.eu/rapid/press-release_SPEECH-17-3165_en.htm. Changes to the Directive have been agreed at the European Council meeting of 23 October 2017.

39 See www.weceurope.org/fileadmin/templates/eurociett/docs/Cross_Border_Activities/Joint_agreement_Eurociett_UNI_on_setting_up_Observatory.pdf.

of outgoing, as opposed to incoming, posted workers are. It is also difficult to measure the real impact – not a very high one in general terms – of posting in national labour markets.[40]

Another innovative example, this time taken from a national experience, can be found in a Dutch collective agreement covering temporary work agencies (Abu Cau 2009–2014), which included in a specific section provisions directed to workers living in the Netherlands on a temporary basis.[41] For this group of workers the possibility of departing from binding norms – for instance with regard to holidays and working time – is envisaged, together with compensation consisting of additional remuneration, so that the overall treatment of posted workers is not pejorative. In addition, the contract offers precise and detailed information with regard to the norms of domestic law which are applicable to workers employed by an agency under the law of a different state.[42]

In other words, a voluntary source, originating from negotiations between private parties, has become the privileged mechanism for the solution of a potential conflict on the applicable law. The social sphere – in this case a collective agreement of a normative and binding character – includes in its own scope temporary workers with a view to anticipating potential controversies. Workers who did not take part in the negotiation and who do not fall within the coverage of the collective agreement in the host state where they reside temporarily are the addressees of a reasonable solution, which is the outcome of a choice made by the social partners to avoid social dumping.

Examples chosen so far confirm that there are several outcomes connected with the suggested theoretical framework of 'transnational juridification'. Solidarity regimes emerge from social spheres which are not necessarily a direct expression of previously aggregated collective interests.

Collective bargaining typically captures the interests of large categories of workers kept together by similar working conditions. New social spheres must interpret the needs and aspirations of mobile workers and

[40] J. Pacolet and D. De Wispelaere, *Posting of Workers. Report on A1b Portable Documents Issued in 2014* (Brussels: European Commission December 2015).

[41] E. Sol and S. Engelsman, *The Netherlands: Temporary Agency Work and Collective Bargaining* (13 January 2009), www.eurofound.europa.eu/observatories/eurwork/comparative-information/national-contributions/netherlands/the-netherlands-temporary-agency-work-and-collective-bargaining.

[42] A new agreement on temporary workers was signed covering the years 2012–2017, www.abu.nl/publicaties/collective_labour_agreement_temporary_agency_workers/files/assets/common/downloads/publication.pdf.

companies and govern the effects of mobility, entering into binding schemes of regulation, characterised by new arrangements supported whenever possible by auxiliary legislation.

A pluralist dimension of solidarity is one of the upshots of restructuring and delocalisation. Social protection in all such cases is directed to weaker individuals or to those who have not been covered by collective agreements or who have not entered other systems of social protection. Standardised tools of protection need to be adapted to changing working environments, which are sometimes temporary and, precisely for this reason, need to be revisited. The principle of equal treatment must govern situations which may seem incomparable, exactly because competitive advantages and social dumping generate them.[43]

In conclusion, in order to track down the steps going towards 'transnational juridification', one needs to ascertain which new aggregations of interests must be taken into account and how supportive legislation can identify such collective interests and protect them through binding measures.

Transnational chains of production offer another example of juridification, whenever the controlling company is in the position to enforce standards throughout the chain. Transnational bargaining is seeking ways to ascertain that fundamental rights are respected by subsidiaries and sub-contractors.

Competitiveness brought about by globalisation of markets indicates that common solutions in fields such as training, work organisation and labour mobility between companies, are missing, whereas they should be complementary to long-term business connections. Especially in the context of a harsh economic crisis, companies tend to be connected in order to intensify the pace of production and answer pressing demands from the market. This shared effort can create conditions of increased stability for workers and also give space for diversifications of work opportunities.

To the contrary, in networks of companies having less strong collaborative relations, consequences in terms of creation of employment opportunities are less visible. Especially in clusters aggregating small and medium enterprises it is unlikely that social partners take action and create the necessary preconditions for collective bargaining.[44] Such clusters could instead be governed by the social partners and generate new levels of

[43] S. Sciarra, 'Notions of solidarity in times of economic uncertainty', *Industrial Law Journal*, 39 (2010), 223 ff.

[44] Eurofound, *Impact of Interfirm Relationships: Employment and Working Conditions* (Luxembourg: Publications Office of the European Union 2011) 55–6, www.Eurofound.europa.eu/pubdocs/2011/01/en/1/EF1101EN.pdf.

collective bargaining, dealing with the peculiarities of geographical areas in which networks of small and medium companies operate.

In the attempt, made so far, to clarify what I have called 'transnational juridification', taking examples mainly from social spheres related to collective bargaining, I suggest that current developments are moving in a double direction.

One development moves outwards, driven by large organisations representing workers, and by multinationals, and aims towards a transnational order of industrial relations, still unclear in its legal foundations, but advancing and looking forward. The second development moves inwards, with the aim of looking at local areas of production, where specific geographical connections exist and where interests could be assembled under the umbrella of organisations willing to enter new levels of collective bargaining. These local chains of production have their own economic relevance and in some cases offer an answer to the crisis.

Large organisations representing employers and workers obey a double allegiance: one towards the states in which they operate and the other one outside of them, depending on the transnational objectives to be pursued. The independence they seek from national legal orders, acting transnationally, does not free them from links to be maintained within established systems of rules. Such is the case for the enforcement of the right to bargain collectively, the right to strike, the active exercise of the rights of information and consultation.

Connections with domestic legal systems are evocative when referred to national and supranational social spheres. The implication is that rights must be enforced at both levels. This double level of enforcement reveals, however, an incomplete process of constitutionalisation, which concerns mainly collective social rights, namely those exercised by organisations representing collective interests. Rights to be exercised collectively are not supported by a shared culture within the EU, despite the fact that they are part of national constitutional traditions. Transnational collective autonomy is searching for more solid foundations and at the same time exploring its potential in the identification of adaptable standards.

Following this perspective, it is extremely pertinent to observe what happens in global law. The programme of the UN 'Global Compact' has accompanied for a long time spontaneous initiatives of large companies, aiming at formalising some practices of corporate social responsibility. An ambitious programme of empirical research and consultation ended up in a Report drafted by John Ruggie, the Special Representative of the

Secretary of the United Nations, dealing with respect for human rights in multinational companies and issuing specific guidelines to companies and states.[45]

The main characteristic of the Ruggie Report is its universality. The objective is to ensure respect for the principles declared by all countries and companies, regardless of their geographical location and independent of their sizes. Principles are organised on the basis of an intelligent combination of national and international measures, binding and voluntary, which should converge towards a coherent system of rules. Companies become ethically as well as legally responsible towards the recipients of their activities, especially if they are headquarters of productive chains connected mainly through economic and organisational relations.

In Principle 12, for instance, reference is made to international sources on civil and political rights and economic, social and cultural rights,[46] as well as to the eight main ILO conventions, referred to in the Declaration on the Fundamental Principles of 1998.[47] Since the responsibility of companies is inspired by the guiding principle of normal diligence, in Principle 17 of the Report it is specified that it is necessary to identify those who are responsible within large productive chains, disseminated around the globe. The value chain, in such cases, risks breaking down if some areas are potentially more exposed, as could happen in chains of sub-contractors. The criteria identified in the Report are, on the one hand, prevention and, on the other, the tracking down of adopted measures through the use of indicators.

The language used in the Ruggie Report is not far from the one adopted in transnational labour law sources, enriched, as we have seen,

[45] J. Ruggie, *Guiding Principles on Business and Human Rights: Implementing the United Nations 'Protect, Respect and Remedy' Framework*, Report of the Special Representative of the Secretary-General on the Issue of Human Rights and Transnational Corporations and Other Business Enterprises, 21 March 2011, for Human Rights Council.

[46] International Covenant on Civil and Political Rights adopted and opened for signature, ratification and accession by General Assembly resolution 2200A (XXI) of 16 December 1966, entry into force 23 March 1976, in accordance with Article 49; International Covenant on Economic, Social and Cultural Rights adopted and opened for signature, ratification and accession by General Assembly resolution 2200A (XXI) of 16 December 1966, entry into force 3 January 1976, in accordance with article 27.

[47] Declaration of ILO on Principles and Fundamental Rights adopted by International Labour Conference during its LXXXVI session in Geneva on 18 June 1998. The adoption of this Declaration marked a new phase in the relationship between the ILO and World Trade Organization, involving the balancing of areas of intervention of the two global organisations.

with references to collective social rights. Rights to information and consultation, the most recently developed among fundamental social rights to be exercised collectively, should become the emblem of a consensual management within large multinational groups of companies and strengthen the right to bargain collectively. Asymmetries in information would be shortened and consensual solutions facilitated.

Affirming the non-subordinate role of social rights with regard to economic freedoms is everything but a purely academic exercise. It is rather a methodological approach, which opens to the establishment of an original nexus between solidarity and competition. Social rights are instrumental to closer market integration and to advanced good practices of coordination among state administrations.

I discuss in the next chapters how, for an improved communication among state administrations and EU institutions, other voices should be better listened to, in particular those of the European Court of Human Rights (ECtHR) and of the ILO. The strong global echo they provoke, wherever fundamental rights are at stake, should be promptly captured in the EU.

4

Conflict and the Uncertain Shape of Transnational Solidarity

Viking and *Laval*

1 Social Rights and Economic Freedoms: A Preliminary Assessment

Issues slowing down market integration and creating a sense of disillusion among European citizens are many and have been acknowledged in the already mentioned Monti Report, as well as in many other policy documents.[1]

This chapter concentrates on a controversial case law of the CJEU, dealing with freedom of establishment and the free provision of services, juxtaposed with the right to strike and to collective bargaining.[2] Controversies were triggered among labour lawyers, even outside the EU, by the Court's exercises in balancing economic freedoms against the right to strike and the right to collective bargaining, giving rise to a heated debate, well beyond a mere academic exercise.

The *Viking* and *Laval* judgments were issued before the entry into force of the Lisbon Treaty, so before the Charter of Fundamental Rights, which fully recognises the fundamental social rights discussed by the Court, acquired the same legal value as the Treaties. After so many years, they are still at the centre of a wide public opinion and remain the emblem of unsolved disputes on how to develop European visions, close to the people of Europe and, at the same time, institutionally sound.

As we will discuss further on, European policy-making provoked by the Court's case law continued to be characterised by strong disagreements, following the issuing by the Commission of the so-called 'Monti II' Council Proposal of Regulation,[3] to be considered a follow-up to an

[1] See Chapter 3.

[2] Literature on this matter is extensive. A comprehensive analysis is in M. Freedland and J. Prassl (eds.), *Viking, Laval and Beyond* (Oxford: Hart Publishing 2014).

[3] European Commission, Proposal for a Regulation on the exercise of the right to take collective action within the context of the freedom of establishment and the freedom to

analogous source, dealing with the functioning of the internal market, issued when Mario Monti was a Member of the European Commission.[4] This attempt was unsuccessful, so much so that in 2013 the Commission had to withdraw the Proposal.[5]

An unsolved tension is at the centre of this prolonged controversy on how to reconcile deeply rooted fundamental social rights, often enshrined in national constitutions, and the opening up of a transnational scene for industrial relations. Large organisations representing employers and workers constantly attempt to adjust their structures, in order to respond to transnational demands coming from their members, with a view to acquiring stronger legitimation and consolidating their power to intervene whenever mobility of companies and workers is at stake.

The evaluation of legal enforceability of collective agreements is equally essential. They are not always endowed with a general *erga omnes* scope; therefore they are not always binding for all workers and employers in each single sector. This, at a first sight merely technical element, mirrors different solutions adopted in domestic legal orders and is extremely relevant for the arguments developed by the CJEU, asked to verify whether solidarity enhanced through collective agreements becomes an obstacle for the efficient functioning of the internal market.

The Court intervened several times to correct the perceived asymmetry between collective social rights and economic freedoms and developed an original – not always straightforward – case law. *Albany*[6] is a most relevant judgment for references made to collective bargaining and its attitude to generate solidarity. In this ruling the Court dealt with a pension fund for textile workers, provided for in a binding collective agreement implemented by a Ministerial Decree.

The Court had to assess that in this case there was not an 'agreement or category of agreements between undertakings' that could restrict or distort competition in the internal market (Article 101.1 TFEU). The Court had also to establish whether social aims pursued by the collective

provide services, COM (2012) 130 final. Comments in Freedland and Prassl (eds.), *Viking, Laval and Beyond,* supra n. 2, 95 ff.

[4] Council Regulation (EC) 2679/98 of 7 December 1998 on the functioning of the internal market in relation to the free movement of goods among the member States (Monti Regulation) OJ L337/8 1998.

[5] See Chapter 5.

[6] C-67/96, *Albany International BV* v. *Stichting Bedrijfspensioenfonds Textielindustrie*, Judgment of the Court of 21 September 1999.

agreement in question entered into conflict with the rules governing the internal market.

In *Albany* the Court avoided delivering a message which would apply to the interpretation of all collective agreements and chose to limit the impact of its own ruling, indicating that the scope and function of collective agreements may differ. Solidarity, an intrinsic precondition and, at the same time, an outcome of collective negotiations, does not make collective agreements automatically immune to the rules of competition law.

This is the background, enriched by other rulings, on which the two controversial cases previously mentioned developed, causing an earthquake in the Court's case law, as well as in the scholarly debate accompanying it. The effects of this profound change for the well-functioning of the internal market were still visible during the drafting of the Monti Report, which devoted attention to them in view of possible policy options.

Viking and *Laval*, for all these reasons, portray a divide in Member States' resilience whenever EU constitutional traditions are at stake. On the one hand rules governing the internal market are imperative and cannot adapt to national industrial relations. Whenever transnational mobility of companies and workers is at stake, recourse to collective actions risks being progressively marginalised. This repercussion of the Court's rulings may induce fear, which easily develops into a destructive criticism, with no alternatives left to reasonable adaptations.

To the contrary, a new supranational scenario could develop, as a direct consequence of the opening up of national legal systems, due to taking into account changes occurring to collective interests represented by large organisations. Accordingly, the right to strike could be included in an integrated system of transnational measures, aimed at avoiding protectionism in the policies put forward by national trade unions.

The inadequacy of merely domestic legal apparatuses for the protection of workers obliges states and social partners to look for different sanctions beyond the state, in parallel with the emersion of new collective interests and of new transnational coalitions.

For labour law, however, linkages with an undefined supranational legal order represent an insurmountable challenge: notions of solidarity are deeply rooted in national traditions and so are the rules governing them. Hence, we may witness harsh competition among different normative systems and, in particular, among wage standards, when transnational interests come to the fore.

This critical assessment of events occurring in the EU, channelled through the CJEU's case law, reveals further complexities when we take into account convergences or divergences between law and collective bargaining. The autonomy of social partners in setting normative standards – a value nourished within national systems of collective bargaining, now acknowledged in Article 152 TFEU – is measured against the urgency to define clear legal standards and ascertain their enforceability in the transnational mobility of companies and workers. This implies adapting principles of equal treatment to workers moved across national frontiers and forging notions of solidarity around such new phenomena.

For all these reasons the role of trade unions is central in the analysis of causes and effects within competing regimes of solidarity, since the transnational relevance of interests to be protected requires new ways to build up legitimacy within collective bargaining.[7]

1.1 Viking: *Conflict in the Seas*

In *Viking* the CJEU entered into a complicated balance of the right to strike, recognised by the Finnish Constitution, with freedom of establishment as regulated by Article 43 of the TEC (now Article 49 TFEU). The description of the facts will allow us to develop the complex and fascinating transnational dimension of maritime work, which has for a long time been at the very centre of highly sophisticated doctrinal and judicial disputes.

A Finnish operator of ferries – the Viking line, which connects Finland and Estonia – was put under severe pressure by Estonian competitors and consequently chose to fly a flag of convenience on the Rosella ferry, in order to apply to its crew lower wages than the ones provided by Finnish collective agreements. Dissociating the flag of the vessel from the nationality of the owner, through a new registration 'of convenience', the operator intended to exercise freedom of establishment within the internal market. Re-flagging the Rosella ferry was a clear manifestation of its intention to move its business to a different Member State and to do so on the ground of primary EU law.

Finnish trade union law provides for the exercise of the right to strike as *extrema ratio*, namely the last step to be taken, following compliance

[7] I have further discussed these issues in S. Sciarra, 'Viking and Laval: collective labour rights and market freedoms in the enlarged EU', in C. Barnard (ed.), *The Cambridge Yearbook of European Legal Studies 2007–2008*, X (Oxford: Hart Publishing 2008), 563 ff. and in 'Notions of solidarity in times of economic uncertainty', *Industrial Law Journal*, 39 (2010), 223 ff.

with the so-called peace obligation, a clause subscribed to by the signatory parties of collective agreements and referred to the sole members included within the scope of such agreements. The peace obligation clause – known also as no-strike clause – is valid and binding, pending the expiration of the agreement and has the function of limiting recourse to industrial action, when the collective agreement is still in force and operating for the definition of terms and conditions of employment.

Viking refused to start new negotiations with the national union active in that particular sector, the Finnish Seamen's Union (FSU), a member of the powerful International Transport Workers' Federation (ITF), since its intention was to lower Finnish wage levels, as a consequence of the change of flag. Such an obstinate refusal provoked the union's reaction and the decision to call the strike. Recourse to industrial action was considered legitimate, because in the meanwhile, when the controversy was still pending, the collective agreement expired and, consequently, the peace obligation ceased to be binding for the parties.

The peculiarities of this case are such that a short detour must be made into union practices in this special field of economic activities and work organisation, in order to frame the dispute and follow the way in which it came to an end.

Since 1948, the year of its foundation in Oslo, ITF has been extremely militant in the fight against flags of convenience, considered one of the priorities of its global mission. This campaign is still active and widespread. In all ports of the world a network of inspectors, made of full-time or part-time union officials, carries the meticulous burden of verifying compliance of collective agreements on vessels.[8]

'Vessels flying flags of convenience' wrote the Swedish labour lawyer Folke Schmidt, a passionate observer of such labour disputes, some decades ago, 'represent a form of capital which is not subject to social control'.[9]

Before the Second World War some small underdeveloped countries, such as Panama, Honduras, Liberia, placed their flags at the disposal of resourceful foreign ship owners, ready to cut off links with social traditions of their countries of origin. 'Countries of convenience' met the

[8] ITF, Flags of convenience campaign, www.itfglobal.org/flags-convenience/index.cfm; N. Lillie, 'Union networks and global unionism in maritime shipping', *Relations industrielles/Industrial Relations*, 60 (2005), 88–111 and N. Lillie, *A Global Union for Global Workers: Collective Bargaining and Regulatory Politics in Maritime Shipping* (New York: Routledge 2006).

[9] F. Schmidt, 'Ships flying flags of convenience', Arkiv for Sjorett (*Journal of Maritime Law*), 12 (1972), 77 and 93.

increasing demand of American and Greek ship owners, whereas Norwegian and Swedish vessels did not follow this practice and kept complying with ILO Recommendation Nos. 107 and 108 of 1958.

The same path was followed by ITF in launching its campaign against flags of convenience, with a view to forcing ship owners to sign collective agreements. ITF followed national traditions when it came to accompanying the campaign with industrial actions, ranging from picketing on US vessels, to dock workers' sympathy strikes in support of seafarers, especially in Sweden. The boycott of vessels whose owners had refused to sign collective agreements and to grant the wages therein laid down, was also a common feature in Finland, Italy, the United Kingdom and Denmark. The legality of all such forms of industrial action was hard to challenge for employers, because of the clear-cut obligations included in collective agreements, driven by powerful organisations representing management and labour.[10]

At the end of this short detour, aimed at offering an historical perspective and revealing the origin of litigation in *Viking*, one can capture the active role played by unions, both at a national and international level. The history of maritime law, on the one hand, and of labour law, on the other, projects a vivid image from the past. In the global strategies pursued by ITF recourse to industrial action proved successful in putting enormous pressure on ship owners and obtaining the expected results in collective negotiations.

However, solidarity among workers throughout different countries is not the right key to use, in order to enter the asymmetries of current industrial relations in the EU. Transnational solidarity, whenever national economies perform differently and labour standards are significantly distant, is not a natural outcome of union cooperation across frontiers. Viking's choice to re-flag Rosella is nothing but an opportunistic market strategy, aimed at seeking advantage in wage dumping.

In this scenario industrial action converts into a contested terrain, since the right to strike is exercised to protect national wage standards and to fight the practice of wage dumping.

Unlike in the campaigns against flags of convenience, where unions were core leaders and international solidarity was being pursued, in *Viking*, and more broadly in controversies framed within the European internal market, courts stand up as the crucial actors and strategies in litigation must necessarily aim at a delicate balancing exercise among social rights and economic freedoms.

[10] Schmidt, supra n. 9, 84–6.

Viking forces us to consider that, when celebrating freedom of establishment in the EU, wage dumping is an option left to ship owners sailing under flags of convenience. The reaction of the Finnish trade union was understandably reported as a way to protect Finnish workers, whose jobs were potentially at risk, following the registration of the ferry in Estonia. These contrasting visions were transferred into a legal action brought by ITF in the Commercial Court in London, where the international union has its headquarters. The British Court of Appeal then made the preliminary reference to the CJEU, after the unions had filed an appeal, following the Court's injunction to limit industrial action.[11]

It is worth mentioning that, because of the initiative taken by a worldwide organisation, litigation acquired a resonance which it might have otherwise not received. The case, however, carried with it resilient symbolic values for the Nordic systems of industrial relations and for the reputation of unions, traditionally inclined to build consensus in efficient systems of collective bargaining.

The prominent role of collective agreements in the Finnish legal order is highlighted in some passages of Advocate General Poiares Maduro's Opinion.[12] First of all he makes a point of excluding analogies with *Albany*,[13] put forward by the applicant unions in an attempt to build a defensive barrier around collective action. He argues that keeping a collective agreement out of the scope of competition rules 'does not necessarily mean that it is also excluded from the scope of the rules on freedom of movement'.[14] It was previously mentioned that *Albany* is, in fact, to be framed within a different sequence of cases, whereby solidarity coincides with the setting up of a pension fund, pursuing a service of general economic interest.

The corollary to this argument is that there is no automatic exemption from the prohibition on restrictions contrary to freedom of establishment (now Article 49 TFEU). Hence, all sorts of collective actions, aimed

11 *Viking Line ABP* v. *International Transport Workers' Federation* [2005] EWCA Civ. 1299, [2006] 1 Lloyd's Rep 303. References to the position taken by trade unions are in B. Bercusson, 'The trade union movement and the European Union: judgment day', *European Law Journal*, 13 (2007), 279 ff.

12 Case C-438/05, *International Transport Workers' Federation and Finnish Seamen's Union* v. *Viking Line ABP e OÜ Viking Line Eesti*, Opinion of 23 May 2007.

13 C-67/96, supra n. 6.

14 *Viking*, Opinion, supra n. 12, paragraph 26. Critical comments in T. Novitz, 'Labour rights as human rights: implications for employers' free movement in an enlarged European Union', in *The Cambridge Yearbook of European Legal Studies 2006–2007*, IX (Oxford: Hart Publishing 2008), 366.

at promoting the objectives of European social policy, may clash with market freedoms: 'Although the Treaty establishes the common market, it does not turn a blind eye to the workers who are adversely affected by its negative traits . . . the European economic order is firmly anchored in a social contract . . . that contract is embodied in the Treaty.'[15]

This conclusion, somehow entrusted by the CJEU in its judgment, prepares the ground for national courts asked to assess whether the right to strike, which is part of general principles of EU law and a constitutional right in Finland, should be limited and restricted, whenever it impedes the exercise of fundamental freedoms guaranteed by the Treaties.

The Court could not omit highlighting that 'the organisation of collective action by trade unions must be regarded as covered by the legal autonomy which those organisations, which are not public law entities, enjoy pursuant to the trade union rights accorded to them, inter alia, by national law'.[16]

Neither could the Court ignore that industrial actions carried out by Finnish trade unions were oriented to the enforcement of collective agreements by the employer and therefore functional to the overall stability of Finnish industrial relations. Primary EU law – the Court maintained – has horizontal direct effect in relationships among private associations, including workers' and employers' organisations.[17]

However, Finnish constitutional values, underpinning relations between management and labour – which substantiate in fundamental social rights such as the right to strike and to bargain collectively – cannot be considered imperative reasons of general interest, the only ones that could justify restrictions to freedom of establishment.

To confirm that collective bargaining aims at protecting collective interests at stake, without imposing excessive burdens on employers, the Court refers to the case law of the ECtHR.[18] Confirming its 'individualistic' approach to freedom of association, in *Wilson* and *Palmer*,[19] the Strasbourg Court did not go as far as including collective bargaining

[15] *Viking*, Opinion, supra n. 12, paragraph 59.

[16] *Viking*, Opinion, supra n. 12, paragraph 35.

[17] *Viking*, Opinion, supra n. 12, paragraph 37: 'collective action such as that described . . . falls, in principle, within the scope of Article 43'. Comments in A. Dashwood, 'Viking and Laval: issue of horizontal direct effect', in *The Cambridge Yearbook of European Legal Studies*, supra n. 7, 525–6.

[18] *Viking*, Opinion, supra n. 12, paragraph 86.

[19] K. Ewing, 'The implications of Wilson and Palmer', *Industrial Law Journal*, 32 (2003), 1 ff.

within the scope of Article 11 ECHR, although it acknowledged that freedom of association is implemented when negotiations start, even though it is not possible to state that this implies a duty to bargain. This reference becomes instrumental in the Luxembourg Court's argument in stating whether or not recourse to collective action is reasonable. The implication is that if it

> goes beyond what is necessary to achieve the objective pursued, it is for the national court to examine, in particular, on the one hand, whether, under the national rules and collective agreement law applicable to that action, FSU did not have other means at its disposal which were less restrictive of freedom of establishment in order to bring to a successful conclusion the collective negotiations entered into with Viking, and, on the other, whether that trade union had exhausted those means before initiating such action.[20]

Hence, the employer's refusal to negotiate can be condemned only by means of industrial action, under typically domestic conditions and practices, bearing in mind the limits set by the Court. Whether collective industrial actions, with a view to protecting employment, are proportional and do not hamper economic freedoms is for the national courts to decide. The conclusion to draw is that *Viking* leads to controversial outcomes, inasmuch as it links the notion of proportionality with interventions of the courts that could hamper the autonomy of private collective parties.[21]

The only way out in a scenario of competing national economies, finally leading to wage dumping, would be to build solidarity among national unions and enhance cooperative agreements. This option, as we shall see, is not totally extraneous to current discussions and policy-making in the transnational posting of workers.[22]

The judicial dispute described so far, following the judgment of the Luxembourg Court, found a solution outside the courtroom, the terms of which the parties preferred to keep confidential.[23] With regard to collective bargaining the outcome was even more innovative at the point that it became an exemplary case applicable also beyond the specific situation.

[20] *Viking*, Opinion, supra n. 12, paragraph 87.

[21] In C-271/08, *European Commission* v. *Federal Republic of Germany*, Judgment of the Court (Grand Chamber) of 15 July 2010, despite a reference to Article 28 of the Charter of fundamental rights, the Court makes a point of referring to *Viking* in order to exclude that collective agreements are immune from rules governing competition in the internal market.

[22] See Chapter 5.

[23] As reported by N. Bruun, 'Finland', in R. Blanpain and A. M. Swiatkowski (eds.), *The Laval and Viking cases: Freedom of Services And Establishment v. Industrial Conflict in the European Economic Area and Russia* (Alphen aan den Rijn: Kluwer 2009), 51.

The European organisations of the sector reached an agreement, taking inspiration from the ILO Convention on maritime work.[24] The Directive implementing the European maritime sector agreement was not to be transposed into the legal systems of Member States before the ratification of the Convention.[25] On 20 August 2013 the Convention entered into force and the event was welcomed by the Commission, who could then proceed, as agreed, with the enforcement of the Directive.

For commentators proposing original solutions in the era of globalisation, this reciprocal contamination among international and European sources raises great interest especially because it signals a consensual exit strategy from a difficult – sometimes unsolvable – competition among normative regimes.

The sector of maritime work, which was analysed, as we have seen above, by respected Scandinavian scholarship in the 1970s, is now open to the attention of the most sceptical observers, to demonstrate that original consensual solutions are possible, notwithstanding the harshness of the judicial controversy. From a more general perspective *Viking* forces commentators to take into account the concrete expansions of transnational and even global labour law, exemplified by the propulsive force of the ILO Convention with regard to an autonomous and private regime of regulation – such as the framework European agreement – then transposed into a Directive.

1.2 Solidarity and Competition: The Court of Justice's Judgment in '3F'

In 2013 the CJEU delivered a relevant judgment,[26] to which we need to refer not so much for the complex procedural issues it implies, but rather for the perspectives it offers with regard to the position of trade unions when they intend to affirm their standing to bring an action and to do so

24 ILO Maritime Labour Convention (C 186), adopted on 23 February 2006. Following the European Commission's consultation of the social partners, a sector agreement was reached on 12 November 2007, which was then transposed into Council Directive 2009/13/EC of 16 February 2009 implementing the Agreement concluded by the European Community Shipowners' Associations (ECSA) and the European Transport Workers' Federation (ETF) on the Maritime Labour Convention, 2006, and amending Directive 1999/63/EC.

25 'This Directive shall enter into force on the date of entry into force of the Maritime Labour Convention, 2006' (Article 7).

26 C-646/11, *3F* v. *European Commission*, Judgment of the Court (Eighth Chamber) of 24 January 2013.

with a view to protecting their role as negotiators. In this perspective, the case at issue constitutes an important precedent, since it reaffirms the need to deepen all implications of solidarity whenever competition law enters the scene.

In order to oppose the practice of 'flags of convenience', Denmark created a register specifically dedicated to ship owners flying the flags of third states (Danish International Ship Owners Register), in addition to the already existing one reserved to national vessels (Danish National Ship Owners Register). Registered international ship owners were admitted to several tax exemptions, limited to them only. These measures allowed flexibility to reduce gross wages, without reducing seafarers' net wages.

These measures prompted 3F, the large Federation of Danish workers which also represents maritime workers, to lodge a complaint in the European Court of First Instance (as it was then called, now named the General Court) on the ground of an alleged omission by the European Commission to open a review procedure and to ascertain whether the measures in question had to be considered state aids. The Court dismissed as inadmissible 3F's application for the annulment of the Commission's Decision, which had found the aids compatible with European law.[27]

The case was then brought to the Court of Justice as an appeal to the Court of First Instance's judgment. The Court of Justice argued that the General Court (of First Instance) had not addressed 3F's arguments, namely to ascertain its competitive position in relation to other trade unions in negotiations of collective agreements applicable to seafarers employed on vessels flying third countries' flags. There were also social implications of the fiscal measures adopted. Hence, the plea of inadmissibility raised by the Commission was rejected and the case went back to the General Court.[28]

The CJEU's ruling, following the appeal by 3F, in rejecting the claim made by the latter – according to which the adoption of fiscal measures in favour of ship owners flying flags of convenience limited its own rights as a negotiator and damaged its members – is very cautious when it comes to exclude collective bargaining from the scope of competition law. Compared to *Albany*, the points made by *3F* suggested an excessively

[27] T-30/03, *SID* v. *Commission*, Judgment of the General Court (Second Chamber, extended composition) of 27 September 2011.

[28] C-319/07, P *3F* v. *Commission of the European Communities*, Judgment of the Court (Third Chamber) of 9 July 2009. ECR I-5963.

broad interpretation of solidarity, since even an indirect effect of fiscal measures is seen as diminishing the right of a trade union to negotiate and bargain collectively. Although the support deriving from the fiscal measure clearly consisted in transferring to ship owners flying flags of convenience a reduction of the wage claims of the seafarers employed, the Court did not delve into the reasons brought by 3F.

However, the Court maintained – and this is the point that we need to highlight – that not granting to a trade union the standing to bring a legal action and to ascertain the exclusion of collective agreements from the scope of competition law, equals precluding the attainment of the objectives of European social policy, enshrined in the Treaty. The Court argued that, in its capacity as a negotiator, the trade union operated on the territory of social policies. *3F* has, in fact, clarified in which way the fiscal measures would have affected the role of negotiator with the ship owners, whose boats were registered in the special register making it plain from a legal perspective the damage to its interests and to the interests of its members.[29]

As it did in *Viking*, the Court in *3F* was seeking a difficult balance between market rules and social policies. The procedural issues at stake in this latter case add a small piece to the puzzle of litigation brought by trade unions on issues of EU law. However, the conclusion of this long controversy came with the 2013 ruling, in which the CJEU dismissed the appeal and ordered 3F to pay the costs.[30]

As anticipated in the opening lines of this chapter, market integration has, in some cases increased the disillusion of European people. To prove the complexity of the reasons behind all such tensions, maritime work has been chosen as a paradigm of conflicting interests and values. Whereas in national legal orders collective bargaining emerged as a direct expression of freedom of association, in the European legal order it is problematic to delimit a space for collective agreements.

A group of experts was required by the Commission to propose solutions, in order to improve the competitiveness of the maritime sector and, at the same time, diminish the risk of social dumping.[31] The experts point to the failures of the so-called Manning Directive – put forward by the Commission in 1998 and withdrawn in 2004 – which should have

[29] C-319/07, *3F* v. *Commission of the European Communities*, supra n. 28, paragraphs 56–7.

[30] Supra n. 26.

[31] Report of the Task Force on Maritime Employment and Competitiveness and Policy Recommendations to the European Commission, 9 June 2011, www.ec.europa.eu/transport/modes/maritime/seafarers/education_en.

imposed comparable standards for maritime workers employed on vessels travelling in European seas and staying in harbours of Member States, in order to prevent the risk of social dumping. Similar risks arise for workers employed in off-shore mobile platforms.

The Commission's attention on these matters was also prompted by the length of procedures for the ratification of the ILO Convention on maritime work, which, as mentioned, was a precondition for the entering into force of the European Directive.

The empty space caused by an inter-institutional fair play, which – at the time of issuing the Report – did not merge two different paths for the implementation of two separate sources – the ILO Convention and the European Directive – pushed the experts towards interlocutory solutions. In fact, they limited themselves to suggesting the improvement of data collection, in order to know better the peculiarities of maritime work and assure equal treatment on vessels based in Member States.

Once more a regulatory conundrum is raised by the attempt to enhance solidarity and competition, amplified by the mobility of workers. The answers provided by the institutions proved to be inadequate and occasionally left space to autonomous initiatives of the social partners. For example, a controversy originating at Irish ferries for a re-flagging of three vessels under the Cypriot flag, gave rise to an out-of-court settlement, reached after signing an agreement. The conclusion was that Latvian workers hired by a Cypriot agency had to be paid at the rate of Irish minimum wage.[32]

One further example can be mentioned, to prove the vast and unpredictable implications of workers' mobility.

In 2009 a dispute arose between Lindsey Oil Refinery and British trade unions, which was also triggered by the lacunas of the posting of workers Directive in a free provision of services. An Italian company, after signing a contract to complete several operations in a refinery owned by the company Total, declared the intention to hire qualified Italian and Portuguese workers for that purpose. The protest of British trade unions exploded in a most violent way, and recourse was made to spontaneous strikes, called with the openly declared intention to protect jobs that

[32] See www.eurofound.europa.eu/observatories/eurwork/articles/irish-ferries-dispute-finally-resolved-after-bitter-stand-off. See also N. Lillie, *The ILO maritime labour convention, 2006: A new paradigm for global labour rights implementation*, in K. Papadakis (ed.), *Cross Border Social Dialogue and Agreements: An Emerging Global Industrial Relations Framework?* (Geneva: International Labour Office 2008).

should only be reserved to British workers, an outcome that had allegedly been guaranteed in a previous agreement.

The potentially discriminatory connotation of industrial action on the ground of nationality should, in this case, be balanced against the impellent urgency of the unions in times of crisis to safeguard in all possible ways local jobs and protect their members. Once more the principle of equal treatment that the Directive on the posting of workers should have pursued in the context of a free provision of services generated unintended consequences. The reference to binding agreements, with a generalised enforceability, found the British unions unprepared and in fact hostile to extending national standards.[33]

The *Lindsey* case was at the centre of a confrontation focused on the slogan 'British jobs for British workers', which was screamed out by workers on strikes and somehow extrapolated from political statements made by the Labour Prime Minister of the time. This episode confirms the contradictions generated by the mere fact that an economic freedom, such as the provision of services, implies the enforcement of fair standards for mobile workers. It also shows a lack of self-discipline in the unions' behaviour.

However, this violent attack on foreign workers did not end up in court. A wiser attitude was shown by the unions in reaching an agreement with Total, with a commitment to create jobs open to British workers, without reducing the number of posted workers.[34]

The *Lindsey* case shows the incomplete and imperfect side of European integration, and a severe attack on solidarity. Its ending, though, is such as to reconcile industrial action with a reasonable and consensual approach.

Formulas adopted are transformative, and sometimes require a compromise. It is important to highlight that strategies proposed by trade unions at a supranational level imply reconsidering the notion of protective measures for workers. Especially with regard to mobility of workers, the risk is to decouple uniform labour standards and diminish the value of comparability among different regimes of solidarity. Protection

[33] C. Kilpatrick, *British Jobs for British Workers? UK Industrial Action and Free Movement of Service in EU Law*, LSE Working Paper, 16/2009; C. Barnard, '"British Jobs for British Workers": The Lindsey oil refinery dispute and the future of local labour clauses in an integrated EU market', *Industrial Law Journal*, 38 (2009), 245 ff.

[34] T. Novitz, 'United Kingdom', in A. Bücker and W. Warneck (eds.) *Viking, Laval, Rüffert: Consequences and Policy Perspectives*, Report 111 (Brussels: European Trade Union Institute 2010), 102–3.

of workers could be rewritten, following the mobility of workers with an aim to defeating the phantom of social dumping.

2 *Laval*: The 'Swedish Model' Under Pressure

Notwithstanding the fact that *Laval* originated from a completely different legal dispute, it is often sided with *Viking* in the narration of a complex story, which sees the Luxembourg Court attempting the interpretation of social rights – collective bargaining and the right to strike – so relevant in the European tradition of trade union law and yet extraneous to its own case law. In the background of this case one can easily detect the contraposition of two very different systems of industrial relations, rooted in unlike traditions of labour markets.

The Swedish system, one of the most solid in the European panorama because of its high rate of union membership, is characterised by a recognised and diffused bargaining power of management and labour organisations. Wage policies are associated with autonomous collective bargaining, with no legal support for collective agreements, since the latter can rely on an extended sphere of enforceability.[35] To the contrary, Latvia, the other country involved in the controversy, was described as the most impoverished European country involved in the enlargement, with a trade union rate of 20 per cent and a downward fluctuation of wage levels, during the transition towards market economy.[36]

The so-called 'Swedish model' was the focus of great attention from European labour law scholarship and from social partners throughout Western countries, especially in the 1970s, when a heated debate on industrial democracy took place in Europe, namely on the enforcement of incisive legal or voluntary measures of workers' control on managerial strategies.

In Sweden auxiliary legislation supported the prerogatives of trade unions and employers' associations. The 1976 'Act on the joint regulation of working life' contributed to the strengthening of the 'Swedish model',

[35] Collective agreements are not universally applicable in Sweden but are de facto widely enforced, because of high membership of the organisations signatories to them. See R. Eklund, T. Sigeman, and L. Carlson, *Swedish Labour and Employment Law: Cases and Materials* (Uppsala: Iustus Förlag 2008), 28 ff.

[36] C. Woolfson and J. Sommers, 'Labour mobility in the construction. European implications of the *Laval un Partneri* dispute with Swedish labour', *European Journal of Industrial Relations*, 12 (2006), 49–68. The authors indicate that in 2004 average wages in countries of enlargement were one-quarter of the average wages in the 'EU 15' Member states.

in which efficient performances of the welfare state and social consensus mixed together in a dynamic combination. It is worth recalling that the 1976 Act, which incorporates and expands provisions of previous laws from 1928 and 1936, was valued in comparative labour law for its sound and well-balanced approach to collective labour rights.[37]

In the Swedish tradition recourse to the right to strike is excluded for disputes on rights – the ones to be settled in court, as they deal with the 'normative' clauses included in collective agreements, binding in individual contracts of employment – but is legal in controversies on interests – the ones dealing with procedural clauses, such as the no-strike clause or peace obligation – mainly related to the functioning of collective bargaining and to negotiations on wages. After the entry into force of the 1976 Act, disputes on interests extended to negotiations preceding the actual bargaining, in order to limit managerial prerogatives that were previously exercised unilaterally. This extension strengthened the role of trade unions in bargaining and consequently shaped the entitlement to industrial actions as a collective one. The unions, not individual workers, were the holders of the right to strike.[38]

In recent years, following similar trends all over the world, the unshakeable Swedish model also showed signs of weakness, in particular for the disaffection towards trade unions. At the beginning of the 1990s, trade union density was around 85 per cent and declined nine percentage points between 1993 and 2005, to reach 76 per cent. In addition, the change of government after the defeat of the social democrats in 2006 accentuated the structural decline of union membership, to reach 72 per cent in 2007.[39] This is not a marginal point to make, in order to contextualise the strong reaction of Swedish trade unions against the Court's judgment.

This detour into some technical and sociological features of the 'Swedish model' aims to describe the social and institutional setting

[37] The English version of the Act, entered into force on 1 January 1977, is in the appendix to F. Schmidt, *Law and Industrial Relations in Sweden* (Stockholm: Almqvist & Wiksell International 1977), 234. An overall assessment of the Swedish system of industrial relations is in F. Schmidt and A. Neal, 'Collective agreements and collective bargaining', in B. Hepple (ed.), *International Encyclopedia of Comparative Law*, XV, Chapter 12 (Tübingen: J.C.B. Mohr 1984).

[38] This point is clearly made in comparative terms by Lord Wedderburn, 'The right to strike: is there a European standard?', in Lord Wedderburn, *Employment Rights in Britain and Europe. Selected Papers in Labour Law* (London, Lawrence and Wishart 1991), 276 ff.

[39] These are the data provided by C. Woolfson, C. Thörnqvist, and J. Sommers, 'The Swedish model and the future of labour standards after *Laval*', *Industrial Relations Journal*, 41 (2010), 335.

within which the dispute between the Latvian company Laval and Swedish trade unions unfolded. In June 2004 the construction company Laval posted some of its workers to Sweden, to take part in the rebuilding of a school in a town close to Stockholm. The posting of workers in the free provision of services was, at the time, dealt with in a European Directive,[40] which has subsequently been amended.[41]

EU law in this field is primarily oriented to enhancing the internal market, hence to facilitating the mobility of companies, with no specific aim to improving social policies or harmonising working conditions of posted workers. The Directive provided that the host state should guarantee to posted workers equal treatment at a minimum protection level provided for in laws and collective agreements having an *erga omnes* enforceability. This is not the case for Swedish collective agreements. A less clear reference in the Directive was to minimum wages, which should have included pay for overtime work, as defined by the host country's national law.

It is not by chance that this last point should become the most controversial in the dispute. In Sweden there is no tradition of minimum wage legislation, since the whole system relies on collective agreements, which are not of general application but become widely enforceable in practice, because they are signed by large representative organisations.

Because of this solid tradition the Swedish legislator, when implementing the Directive, had not provided for a universal extension of collective agreements with regard to wages, despite a clear provision in the Directive.

Laval at first refused recourse to a special clause in the collective agreement, which allows employers, foreign ones as well, which are not members of the signatory organisation, to apply the plant level collective agreement and to guarantee compliance with the peace obligation clause. Such a clause provides that no industrial action takes place if the agreement is still in force.

It is likely that the high wage level that would have become applicable to the workers posted in Sweden induced Laval's refusal.[42] It is also

40 Directive 96/71/EC of the European Parliament and of the Council of 16 December 1996 concerning the posting of workers in the framework of the provision of services.

41 Directive 2014/67/EU of the European Parliament and of the Council of 15 May 2014 on the enforcement of Directive 96/71/EC concerning the posting of workers in the framework of the provision of services and amending Regulation (EU) No. 1024/2012 on administrative cooperation through the Internal Market Information System ('the IMI Regulation') currently undergoing further revisions.

42 Woolfson and Sommers, supra n. 36, 54, mention that a refusal to sign decentralised collective agreements is frequent for non-Swedish companies. This confirms the non-cooperative attitude of Swedish unions against such companies.

possible that the Swedish liaison office, which, according to the Directive, should have facilitated release of information to foreign service providers, was not as efficient as expected.[43] The details emerging from the facts originating in the dispute are many and all controversial. The Court does not hide its disappointment in pointing to Laval's refusal to sign, although it has to delve into the details of the negotiations on applicable wages for the construction sector. This obstinate refusal may have contributed to a deterioration in the relationship with the unions, up to the point that the union organising workers of the electricity sector called a strike in sympathy with workers in the construction sector. It was this secondary industrial action which, as we read in between the lines of the judgment, blocked all activities in the building site and originated Laval's legal action before the Swedish labour court, claiming that the strike should be declared illegal and damages should be quantified.

The preliminary ruling filed by the Swedish court to the CJEU originated from the bad functioning of negotiations, which then triggered the industrial action. The concrete exercise of the right to strike, in particular the blockage of the building site, could be in breach of Article 56 TFEU, since freedom to provide services was jeopardised. The reluctance of the liaison office to release prompt and clear information needs also to be recalled, in view of understanding further developments. The integration of the internal market through the free mobility of companies providing services is also structured around cooperation among national administrations. Duties to inform and to act transparently are as relevant as the guarantee to exercise economic freedoms.

The dialogue of the Swedish court with the court in Luxembourg was not an easy one. There was a distance in the language, which reflected the peculiarities of the 'Swedish model' and mirrored some intrinsic difficulties in transmitting the culture of industrial relations, so deeply rooted in national traditions.

The Court, notwithstanding the numerous references in the Advocate General's Opinion, who acknowledged the right to strike as part of European labour law traditions, did not manage to elaborate an interpretation of the same that could be balanced with the freedom to provide services. Accordingly, the Court oriented its judgment to favouring the exercise of economic freedoms, disregarding social rights, which should impede an unfair competition between foreign companies and the ones based in the host state.

[43] *Laval*, paragraphs 9 and 35.

The lack of measures such as arbitration or any other alternative dispute resolution, added to the non-binding enforceability of collective agreements, makes the choice of the foreign service provider merely optional, when it comes to applying minimum labour standards and in particular minimum wages.[44]

Social dumping is, in this perspective, much more than a mere theoretical assumption. It emerges as the paradoxical result of a national self-concluded system of collective bargaining, not connected to other external systems. Hence, transnational mobility of companies and labour does not match with national labour standards. Since the right to strike has in the Swedish system an instrumental function to collective bargaining, it acts as a peculiar sanction within national bargaining procedures and, in particular, only with regard to disputes on interests.

Self-determination of the unions is a national character, not easy to grasp for a supranational court, which includes judges coming from different legal cultures and speaking different languages.[45] The most intuitive technique for the Court to adopt – but a controversial one in this case – is resorting to the principle of proportionality.[46] The imperative reasons of general interest were not considered so resilient to justify a limitation to the economic freedom, if such a limitation makes the objective pursued by the Treaty unattainable.[47]

The exclusion of the right to strike from the competences of the Treaty (Article 153 paragraph 5 TFEU) does not diminish its potential collision with a fundamental freedom (Article 56 TFEU) when it is exercised beyond the limits proportionally compatible with the free provision of

[44] *Laval*, paragraphs 68–76. In C-346/06, *Dirk Rüffert* v. *Land Niedersachsen*, Judgment of the Court (Second Chamber) of 3 April 2008, the Court maintains that minimum wages only, without references to other additional elements, can be imposed to the service provider, in order to avoid infringements of Article 56 TFEU.

[45] F. Mancini, 'Language, culture and politics in the life of the European Court of Justice', now in *Democracy and Constitutionalism in the European Union* (Oxford: Hart Publishing 2000), 192.

[46] *Laval*, paragraphs 93–103, with references to Case C-112/00, *Eugen Schmidberger, Internationale Transporte und Planzüge* v. *Republik Österreich*, Judgment of the Court of 12 June 2003 and Case C-36/02, *Omega Spielhallen- und Automatenaufstellungs-GmbH* v. *Oberbürgermeisterin der Bundesstadt Bonn*, Judgment of the Court (First Chamber) 14 October 2004, which the Court, however, does not follow.

[47] See on this point Case C-319/06, *Commission of the European Communities* v. *Grand Duchy of Luxemburg*, Judgment of the Court (First Chamber) of 19 June 2008, where the Court amplifies this concept. See also the judgment of the EFTA Court dealing with the law of Iceland on posted workers: *EFTA Surveillance Authority* v. *Iceland*, of 28 June 2011, E-12/10, paragraph 56.

services. Article 56 – as was previously mentioned in *Viking*, with regard to Article 49 TFEU – is sanctioned with horizontal effectiveness, also with regard to private organisations representing collective interests.

In addition, the Court in *Laval* had to explore an anomaly of the Swedish legal system. The so-called *Lex Britannia*, adopted in 1991 with the objective of fighting dumping, entered into force as a reverberation of a controversy between a ship owner, flying a flag of convenience, and the Swedish unions of the sector. The law provided that there was no violation of the peace obligation – the clause in collective agreements according to which unions should not call a strike when collective agreements have not yet expired – and industrial action was legitimate when the latter was addressed to a foreign employer temporarily active in Sweden in order to make him sign and enforce the collective agreement. The Court declared this provision discriminatory on the ground of nationality, contrary as such to European law.[48]

It is not within the scope of this chapter to comment on all details of this complex judgment, which emerges, from the short account given so far, as an unusual interplay between the interpretation of EU law and the attempt to understand the many complexities of Swedish trade union law.[49] Similarly to what happened in the follow-up to the *Viking* case, the main point to be made is to highlight the extraordinary 'snowball' effect put in action by the Luxembourg Court on delicate issues related to collective social rights. Beyond the evaluation of the technicalities involved in balancing social rights and economic freedoms in the context of EU law, we need to connect each single case to a wider context of international law. This analysis will be proposed in the next chapter, when selected cases decided by the ECtHR will be discussed.[50]

It is now time to look at what happened after *Laval*, and consider its effects and implications, which went well beyond the Swedish legal

[48] *Laval*, paragraphs 116 ff. This law was revised, following the *Laval* judgment.

[49] Some early comments concentrated on the peculiarities of the national legal systems under discussion. For example, R. Eklund, 'A Swedish perspective on *Laval*', *Comparative Labor Law and Policy Journal*, 29 (2008), 551 ff. and G. Orlandini, 'Trade union rights and market freedoms: European Court of Justice sets out the rules', *Comparative Labor Law and Policy Journal*, XXIX, 4 (2008) 573 ff. See also N. Reich, 'Free movement v social rights in an enlarged Union: the "Laval" and "Viking" cases before the European Court of Justice part I and II', *German Law Journal*, 9 (2008), 125–60, static1.squarespace.com/static/56330ad3e4b0733dcc0c8495/t/5761e7e3c534a595c6d17872/1466034148824/GLJ_Vol_09_No_02.pdf.

[50] See Chapter 5.

system. The urgency of watching beyond national borders is triggered not only by economic reasons but also by new perspectives in integrating solidarity regimes.

2.1 A 'Snowball' Effect: Lawmakers and Judges after Laval

Laval prompted several transformations in national legal systems and could still be at the origin of other radical changes within the EU. We will look only to some of the issues, which confirm the unpredictable 'snowball effect' of a judgment. Reasons for this unusual resonance are to be found in the linkages keeping together national legal systems within a single market. However, the delicate implications of matters involving national constitutional traditions – social rights and the autonomy of social partners – originated an even wider reaction, calling for the comparison between EU law and international standards. Let us start with the first visible impact of *Laval* in the Scandinavian countries.

The Danish government appointed a committee, charged to study and propose changes to the legislation regulating the posting of workers in the free provision of services. It was a rapid and provident move, almost a preventive measure aimed at preserving the salient qualities of the national system of collective bargaining.[51]

The first change introduced in Denmark concerned the right to strike, considered legitimate only when addressed to obtain wage treatments equivalent to the ones applied by Danish employers for equivalent activities carried out by posted workers. The other legislative intervention concerned the principle of transparency recalled in *Laval*, whereby a precondition for the legitimate exercise of the right to strike is a clear reference to collective agreements signed by the most representative social partners and to the wage treatment there included.[52]

The Danish legislator aimed, with this reference, to recall Article 3 paragraph 8 of Directive 96/71, because in that system, as in Sweden, minimum wages are defined in collective agreements without general enforcement *erga omnes*. The amendments entered into force on 1

[51] The Report issued by the Government Committee, published in June 2008, is commented by R. Nielsen, 'Denmark', in Blanpain and Swiatkowski (eds.), *The Laval and Viking cases*, supra n. 23, 25 ff.

[52] N. Bruun, C-M. Jonsson, and E. Olauson, 'Consequences and policy perspectives in the Nordic countries as a result of certain important decisions of the Court of Justice of the EU', in A. Bücker and W. Warneck (eds.), *Reconciling Fundamental Social Rights and Economic Freedoms after Viking, Laval and Rüffert* (Baden Baden: Nomos 2011), 32–3.

January 2009, thus confirming the efficiency of the Danish system open to necessary and urgent changes.

Danish social partners also gave a signal of change with the same prompt attitude. In March 2011 an agreement entered into force signed by the employer association DHV and by the large federation 3F, providing the obligation for affiliated construction companies to contract out activities only to undertakings applying sector collective agreements. Although this agreement lacks a clause of shared liability, it provides for a sanction against whoever violates the agreement. The choice to enter collective bargaining is, once more, preferred to legislative intervention in the fight against social dumping.[53]

As for Sweden, in April 2008 the Government charged the Director of the national office of mediation with the task of carrying out and coordinating an investigation on the amendments to be adopted in order to change national law, in compliance with the *Laval* judgment. In December 2008 a committee, composed of three experts, published a report, after having consulted the social partners and a large number of labour law scholars throughout the Scandinavian countries, having also received the opinion of the Swedish authority for the control of working life.[54]

The committee dealt with all controversial issues raised by *Laval*, ranging from the discriminatory contents of the *Lex Britannia* to the amendments to be introduced to the law transposing the Directive on the posting of workers, including the general scope of collective agreements and, more widely, the core of the mandatory rules to be applied to posted workers. The latter were needed to clarify the uncertain notion of 'public order' contained in Article 3 paragraph 10 of Directive 97/71, since only mandatory rules characterising the core of protective measures addressed to workers can be included in such a definition and be excluded from clashes with Article 56 TFEU.

The committee's report paved the way to the legislator that accepted almost completely the proposals and modified the Swedish law, following the CJEU's judgment. The new '*lex Laval*'[55] changed the rules implementing the Directive and the already mentioned 1976 Act on the joint regulation of working life. The exercise of the right to strike was made

[53] K. Pedersen, 'New agreement to combat social dumping', *Eurofound online*, 10 June 2011, www.Eurofound.europa.eu/eiro/2011/03/articles/dk1103019i.htm.

[54] The Committee, chaired by C. Stråth, issued a Report, available in a short English version: *Action in Response to the Laval judgment* (Stockholm: Swedish Government Official Reports, 2008).

[55] Law No. 228/2010, entered into force on 15 April 2010.

subject to legal limits, whenever the collective action aims to obtain from foreign providers of service the signing of a collective agreement. Minimum working conditions, also with regard to wages to be applied to posted workers, are the ones included in collective agreements at a centralised level.

It was held unlawful to call a strike if the working conditions applicable to foreign providers of services were equivalent to the conditions applied in Sweden. The burden of proof with regard to the conditions applied is, in any case, on the company posting the workers. This last amendment was among the most controversial changes, because it introduced a problematic comparison between different normative standards emerging from the reference to domestic systems of collective bargaining. It is also for this reason that some Swedish trade unions manifested the doubt that some collective agreements exhibited by foreign companies to prove the contractual conditions applied could be forged.[56]

In this new regulatory framework further visibility was assigned to the Swedish authority for the control of working life, identified as the national contact point, namely the office within the national administration responsible, according to the Directive, for the release of transparent information to service providers interested in operating in Sweden. Typically, this should be yet another example of cooperation between national administrations, which should increasingly facilitate the integration of the internal market.

Messages sent by the Swedish legislator in the aftermath of *Laval* required the state to fully observe the obligations stemming from membership of the EU and trade unions to have a responsible attitude in preventing social dumping. The answer to the CJEU had these two trajectories. However, the story does not end there.

The 'snowball effect' caused by *Laval* had another consequence which must be pointed out. In December 2009 the Swedish labour court issued a judgment on the action for damages started by the Latvian construction company against Swedish trade unions.[57]

[56] N. Bruun and J. Malmberg, 'Sanctions for "EU unlawful" collective action', in S. Evju (ed.) *Regulating Transnational Labour in Europe: The Quandaries of Multilevel Governance* (Oslo University Press 2014), 214 ff.

[57] The judgment of the Labour court No. 89/2009, in an unofficial English version, is available at www.arbetsratt.juridicum.su.se/Filer/PDF/ErikSjoedin/AD%202009%20nr%2089%20Laval%20English.pdf. The Swedish Labour court is both the first and last instance court for a large number of labour law disputes, including the ones on the right to strike. The Court is tripartite.

Arguing on the ground of the CJEU's judgment, despite the absence of a precise reference in Swedish law regulating the regime of liability for the breach of primary EU law, the labour court condemned the unions to the payment of punitive damages. Since the quantification of the damage was not straightforward, Swedish judges decided to inflict on trade unions an exemplary penalty, not so much for the amount to be paid but rather for the ground-breaking legal precedent it created.[58]

This case is a peculiar one for many reasons. The labour court used a national parameter, namely a sanction provided in Swedish law for illegal strikes, to assess a collective action exercised in contrast with EU law. In addition – and this is an element which adds even more to the gravity of the episode from a systematic perspective – the Court did not refer the case to Luxembourg in view of a preliminary ruling, to assess the liability of the state for the imprecise implementation of the Directive. Rather than using the liability of the state and assessing retroactively the amount of damages due to Laval, the Court found the unions liable for having exercised the right to strike lawfully, according to Swedish law, but with a sufficiently clear violation of European law. Hence, damages were issued on the ground of an analogy with the provisions of the 1976 Co-determination Act, without an in-depth investigation into the state's liability.[59]

This unusual and controversial hybridisation of remedies resulted in a majority decision, with three of the seven judges writing dissenting opinions. However, some commentators welcomed the judgment as a more effective form of protection of economic freedoms, useful to fill a gap in the European legal system, therefore to be extended to similar cases through analogy.[60] It is to be ascertained whether this debatable precedent should have a follow-up, outside of Sweden. It certainly shows the anxiety of the Swedish labour court in making a strategic use of EU law – if not a proper abuse of the same – in order to solve a domestic problem.

The judgment is, in fact, an inadequate reading of the CJEU's case law on direct effect of primary EU law with regard to private parties, such as

[58] Damages amounted to 555,000 Swedish crowns, approximately 60,500 euros.

[59] M. Rönnmar, 'Sweden', in Freedland and Prassl (eds.), *Viking, Laval and Beyond*, supra n. 2, 249. More generally, see R. Zahn, *New Labour Law in Old Member States* (Cambridge University Press 2017).

[60] U. Bernitz and N. Reich, 'The Labour Court, Sweden (Arbetsdomstolen) Judgment No. 89/09 of 2 December 2009, *Laval un Partneri Ltd v Svenska*', *Common Market Law Review*, 48 (2011), 615.

the unions, external to the administration of the state. The private and autonomous configuration of the unions must be strongly defended, since it qualifies their action independently from the state. For this reason, the expansion through analogy of the principle of liability for breach of EU law, proposed by the Swedish labour court, is questionable.[61]

Criticism addressed to this decision is also based on the assumption that threats inflicted against large organisations representing collective interests may result in restrictions or even impediments in the exercise of social rights, unless the denunciation of illegal actions is soundly supported. The horizon opening up after *Laval* should not have been defined through judicial strategies, particularly when they result in intrusive measures against private parties. The alternative prediction should have been building up consensual strategies, through collective bargaining, and the identification of convergences at transnational level, in order to propose comparable labour standards, when transnational mobility of companies and workers occurs.

The largest Swedish confederations were unhappy with the outcome of this long saga. *Lex Laval* limited consistently their prerogatives and clashed with the Swedish tradition of equal treatment in working conditions. The strategy, this time, was constructed with references to international standards.

The 2012 ILO Report delivered by the Committee of Experts on the Application of Conventions and Recommendations (CEACR) found that the post-*Laval* legislation adopted in Sweden lacked measures on proportionality that should apply whenever the right to strike is balanced against economic freedoms. Similar concerns were expressed with regard to collective bargaining, since the law limited the autonomy of the unions in setting the contents of agreements to be signed by foreign service providers. There was also an issue of freedom of association for workers posted to Sweden, since they had to be put in the position to choose freely their representatives. Hence, the Swedish government was solicited to review the law entered into force in 2010 and to do so in accordance with the social partners.[62]

[61] Reference made by the labour court to Case C-94/07, *Andrea Raccanelli* v. *Max-Planck-Gesellschaft zur Förderung der Wissenschaften eV*, Judgment of the court (Fifth Chamber) 17 July 2008 is debatable. Contra Bernitz and Reich, supra n. 60, 609.

[62] International Labour Conference, 102nd Session 2013, Report of the Committee of Experts on the Application of Conventions and Recommendations, Part II, 176–80.

The Swedish Trade Union Confederation (LO) and the Confederation of Professional Employees (TCO) took the initiative to lodge a collective complaint to the Committee of Experts monitoring the enforcement of the ESC. The complaint is meticulously drafted in its twofold structure. Starting from the assumption that collective labour rights were imperilled by the *Lex Laval*, the complaint points to the significant limits introduced to collective bargaining and the right to take industrial action (Article 6 paragraphs 2 and 4 ESC). Furthermore, the same collective labour rights must be recognised to migrant workers, who are also entitled to decent wages, when they move to a host country (Article 19 paragraph 4(a)–(b) ESC).[63]

The expansion of legal solutions beyond EU law is convincing and so is the answer offered by the Experts, who consider the ESC a distinct system of norms, without a presumption of conformity with EU law. This is a proposition of self-restraint and inter-institutional fair play. Nevertheless, the impact of the Committee's Decision on the Swedish government is noteworthy, and so is its resonance in the international arena. The Experts acknowledge that economic freedoms play a role in the internal market and are guaranteed by EU law. However, they clarify that such freedoms 'cannot be treated, from the point of view of the system of values, principles and fundamental rights embodied in the Charter, as having a greater *a priori* value than core labour rights, including the right to collective action to demand further and better protection of the economic and social rights and interests of workers'.[64]

It is worth mentioning that, in the meanwhile, the Directive on posted workers was modified[65] and the CJEU delivered a judgment which opens new perspectives in guaranteeing equal treatment to posted workers.[66]

We are approaching the end of the story, or if you like we are entering the valley where the snowball stops its frenetic tour. On 1 June 2017 the 'New posting regulation' entered into force in Sweden, following an inquiry into the enforcement of the *Lex Laval*.[67] The legislator is, this

[63] Complaint No. 85/2012 *Swedish Trade Union Confederation (LO) and Swedish Confederation of Professional Employees (TCO)* v. *Sweden*. The Decision of the European Committee of Social Rights was delivered on 3 July 2013.

[64] Decision, supra n. 63, paragraph 18. [65] Directive 2014/67, supra n. 41.

[66] C-396/13, *Sähköalojen ammattiliitto ry* v. *Elektrobudowa Spolka Akcyjna*, Judgment of the Court (First Chamber) 12 February 2015.

[67] *Lag (2017:320)* modifies *Lag (1999:678) om utstationering av arbetstagare* (Posting of Workers Act 1999:6789, previously amended by the *Lex Laval*). An early comment: K. Ahlberg, 'Lex Laval revised in Sweden – to what effect?', www.nordiclabourjournal .org/nyheter/news-2017/article.2017–03-01.0991266340.

time, driven by the intention to avoid the exploitation of posted workers and to encourage collective bargaining. The foreign service provider should, if requested, appoint a representative to carry on negotiations and conclude collective agreements. Industrial action is lawful when aimed at achieving a collective agreement for posted workers, in order to apply minimum conditions under Swedish sector agreements.

The first impression is that impulses coming from outside the EU were momentous and produced a reconsideration of previous decisions. The interdependence of legal sources applying transnationally does not diminish the scope of EU law, as long as national legislators are aware of parallel implications deriving from their membership in international organisations.

The recurring idea, put forward in these pages, consists in the search for alternatives to social dumping, through the construction of transnational regimes of solidarity. Resort to conflict could paradoxically accentuate differences among stronger and weaker actors, without creating the preconditions for solidarity. However, the right to strike continues to be inscribed among the fundamental values recognised in international sources and well-grounded in national constitutional traditions.

5

Voices from Global Law

1 The Strasbourg Court and Freedom of Association

The judgments in *Viking* and *Laval* issued by the Luxembourg Court shocked the global legal order and provoked a confrontation from a distance with the Strasbourg Court when the latter decided *Demir and Baykara*[1] and *Enerji Yapi-Yol Sen.*[2]

Both decisions are grounded on the interpretation of freedom of association, as for Article 11 of the ECHR. They show a new emphasis put by the Court on issues dealt with in its previous case law.[3]

Professor Lord Wedderburn, whose scholarly work crossed the boundaries of European and international labour law for some decades, was among the most disenchanted interpreters of Article 11. His inclination to comparative labour law induced him to point out different implications connected with the actual exercise of freedom of association, read in parallel with the right to organise, with special attention to the case law of the ECtHR developed around the mid-1970s and continued in subsequent decisions.[4] Article 11 does not refer expressly to collective bargaining, when it deals with the right to form and join a trade union.

1 European Court of Human Rights, *Demir and Baykara* v. *Turkey*, Application No. 34503/97, Grand Chamber, 12 November 2008.

2 European Court of Human Rights, *Enerji Yapi-Yol Sen* v. *Turkey*, Application No. 68959/01, 21 April 2009.

3 It is worth recalling the text of ECHR, Article 11 'Freedom of assembly and association' '1. Everyone has the rights to freedom of peaceful assembly and to freedom of association with others, including the rights to form and to join trade unions for the protection of his interests. 2. No restrictions shall be placed on the exercise of these rights other than such as are prescribed by law and are necessary in a democratic society in the interests of national security or public safety, for the prevention of disorder or crime, for the protection of health or morals or for the protection of the rights and freedoms of others. This Article shall not prevent the imposition of lawful restrictions on the exercise of these rights by members of armed forces, of the police or of the administration of the State.'

4 Lord Wedderburn, 'Freedom of association or right to organize? The common law and international sources', in *Employment Rights in Britain and in Europe: Selected Papers in Labour Law* (London: Lawrence and Wishart 1991), 138 ff.

Hence, the Court maintained that this was only one of the possible measures guaranteed under the wide notion of freedom of association and did not imply specific obligations for the states in support of collective bargaining.[5]

Article 11 paragraph 1 was interpreted by the ECtHR to give additional value to the negative freedom of association, namely the right held by individuals not to form a union and not to join it. This was a turning point in the case law of the Strasbourg Court, of great relevance for national legal systems – in particular the British one – in which access to the benefits connected with collective bargaining was conditional upon membership of the unions through a 'closed shop' agreement.[6]

Lord Wedderburn was critical of the individual dimension of freedom of association developed in the approach taken by the ECtHR and opposed, in his analysis, the structural difference of the ILO sources, historically open to include measures for the protection of collective rights. During the 1970s, comparative research encouraged the attitude of legislators in Western countries to provide legal support for the enforcement of union rights and to strengthen the collective dimension of freedom of association.[7]

In *Demir and Baykara* the ECtHR was presented with the case of trade unions in the public sector, claiming that their right to collective bargaining had been infringed. The Court offered a systematic interpretation of Article 11, which expanded its previous rulings. It started from the assumption that, in order to grant protection of human rights, not in a merely theoretical or illusory manner, the ECHR should be placed in the context of a general system of international law, understood as a living and constantly evolving body of norms.[8] The rule of law is not jeopardised, neither is a predictable interpretation put at risk, if Article 11 is

[5] Among some most relevant cases see: *Swedish Engine Drivers' Union* v. *Sweden*, Application No. 5614/72, 6 February 1976; *Schmidt and Dashlström* v. *Sweden*, Application No. 5582/72, 6 February 1976; *Rolf Gustavson* v. *Sweden*, Application No. 23196/94, 1 July 1997; *Wilson, National Union of Journalists and others* v. *United Kingdom*, Application Nos. 30668/96, 30671/96 and 30678/96, 2 July 2002.

[6] Lord Wedderburn, *The Worker and the Law* (Harmondsworth: Penguin Books 1986), 376 ff., critical of the ECtHR in *Young, James, Webster* v. *United Kingdom*, Application No. 7601/76, 7806/77, 13 August 1981.

[7] O. Kahn-Freund, *Labour and the Law* (London: Stevens & Sons 1977), 166 ff. Kahn-Freund was also a scrupulous interpreter of the Council of Europe's Social Charter, which includes the right to strike among collective social rights. O. Kahn-Freund, 'The European Social Charter', in F. J. Jacobs (ed.) *European Law and the Individual* (Amsterdam: North Holland Publisher 1976), 181 ff.

[8] *Demir*, supra n. 1, paragraphs 66–8.

interpreted broadly, including in it the right to collective bargaining, in line with an evolving interpretation in global law.[9]

In *Enerji Yapi-Yol Sen* v. *Turkey*[10] the ECtHR discussed the ban, contained in a document circulated by the Presidency of the Council and directed to the employees, to join a strike called by the national federation of public workers, to support the right to collective bargaining. The infringement of Article 11 was unmistakable in the Court's view, particularly in the light of ILO sources. The Court mentions its previous judgment in *Demir*, maintaining that the right to strike also falls within the scope of freedom of association, inasmuch as it is supportive of the right to collective bargaining.

Limits to the right to strike, which the Court acknowledges, are subject to a restrictive interpretation of Article 11 and concern only specific categories of public employees, whose functions are identifiable as a direct expression of state powers. This interpretation is broad enough to cover paragraphs 1 and 2 of Article 11, with the intention to highlight that states are bound to attentively justify restrictions to a fundamental human right such as the right to strike.[11]

In the new approach followed by the Strasbourg Court, an interpretation of freedom of association as the expression of individual choices, gives way to a collective vision of the same, grounded more clearly on collective bargaining and the right to strike, both concerned with enhancing collective interests. The step taken by the Court is far from being negligible and should be assessed in its broad implications, especially for the intention to impose respect for human rights in a country like Turkey, which was at the time of the judgments a reliable candidate to join the EU.

The case law of the ECtHR inevitably enters into competition with the CJEU's judgments in *Viking* and *Laval*. As much as this can be seen as a positive impulse for the EU, it also raises worried comments.[12] The

[9] *Demir*, supra n. 1, paragraphs 153–4. Judge Zagrebelsky's separate opinion points to the potential implications of the judgment, as for the retroactive effect of the same. Hence, the point made in paragraph 154 raises the question on the temporal effect of the right to collective bargaining, as part of the enforcement of Article 11 ECHR.

[10] *Enerji*, supra n. 2.

[11] Following these two leading cases, the ECtHR delivered other judgments in which it confirmed its interpretation. In *Saime Özcan* v. *Turkey*, Application No. 22943/04, 15 September 2009; *Kaya and Seyhan* v. *Turkey*, Application No. 30946/04, 15 September 2009 the Court dealt again with the right to strike and to its full enforcement, without interferences that might deter unions from starting the action.

[12] Comments in K. D. Ewing and J. Hendy, 'The dramatic implications of Demir and Baykara', *Industrial Law Journal*, 39 (2010), 2–51. The Court of Justice should reconsider

metaphor of the two European courts engaged in a dialogue fades away and the merging of the two systems of norms seems, for the moment, postponed.

The clear statement made in Article 6 paragraph 2 TEU indicates that accession to the ECHR shall not affect the Union's competences 'as defined in the Treaties' thus implying that the separation of sources on which the two courts exercise their jurisdiction remains unchanged.[13] The convergence of standards is, therefore, left to autonomous interpretations of the two courts and subject to changes in the case law.[14]

2 Conflict in the Skies: A Voice from Geneva

Before the judgment of the ECtHR in *Demir* was delivered, a British case was submitted to the ILO CEACR, an independent body in which competence and experience must prevail on political affiliations.

The British union of pilots (BALPA) called a strike to protest against British Airways' decision to open a subsidiary called Open Skies, committed to the handling of flights between European countries and the United States. This decision was taken, according to the union, without taking into account its potential impact on employment in the United Kingdom. British Airways declared its intention to request an injunction and started an action for damages, relying on the CJEU's rulings in *Viking* and *Laval*. It held that the strike called by the union organising pilots was illegal, since it collided with the company's economic freedom. The possibility, deemed likely, that the British Court would refer the case to the CJEU had a sufficiently high deterrent impact on the union's decision, so much so that the industrial action was called off.[15]

its own case law, taking into account the ECtHR's judgments, according to T. Novitz, 'Collective action in the United Kingdom', in E. Ales and T. Novitz (eds.), *Collective Action and Fundamental Freedoms in Europe. Striking the Balance* (Antwerp, Intersentia 2010), 173 ff.

[13] Protocol No. 8 relating to Article 6(2) of the Treaty on European Union on the accession of the Union to the European Convention on the Protection of Human Rights and Fundamental Freedoms, attached to the Lisbon Treaty.

[14] In *National Union of Rail, Maritime and Transport Workers* v. *United Kingdom* Application No. 31045/10, 8 April 2014 the ECtHR recognised a consistent margin of appreciation to the state in provisions regarding the ban of secondary actions. Comments in A. Bogg and K. D. Ewing, 'The implications of the RMT case', *Industrial Law Journal*, 43 (2014), 221 ff.

[15] References in the country report by T. Novitz, 'United Kingdom', in A. Bücker and W. Warneck (eds.), *Viking, Laval, Rüffert: Consequences and Policy Perspectives*, Report 111 (Brussels, European Trade Union Institute 2010), 103.

The point can be made that one of the parties involved in the dispute, British Airways, had a powerful tool to rely on when it threatened a preliminary reference to the CJEU. Pressure on the union was such to pre-empt industrial action even before a concrete exercise of the right to strike took place.

BALPA, conscious of this anomalous asymmetry in the industrial dispute, chose to direct its protest to the CEACR, pointing to the violation of the ILO Convention No. 87.[16] CEACR, acting with institutional fair play, did not go as far as entering into the technicalities of the CJEU's rulings and evaluating their soundness. It merely assessed the possibility of a negative impact on the exercise of the rights included in Convention No. 87. British Airways, therefore, succeeded in threatening the union, with an aggressive behaviour.

The relevant point to make is that this attack on a fundamental right was grounded on references to judgments of a court exercising its jurisdiction on EU law and ruling on references originated in completely different legal circumstances. Resort to industrial action was impeded on the assumption that economic losses for the union would be unsustainable, had there been an order to pay damages.[17]

The British government, intervening in the dispute, underlined the national dimension of the conflict at issue and the possibility to resort only to sanctions provided by the domestic legal system. Such a system should not be compared to the EU system and to the law enhancing economic freedoms.

With a clever answer, CEACR pointed to the fact that in a global context the interdependence of rulings delivered by different courts, in different jurisdictions, will become more frequent and will be so especially in the transport sector.[18]

[16] Application by the British Air Line Pilots Association to the International Labour Organisation Committee of Experts on the Application of Conventions and Recommendations against the United Kingdom for breach of ILO Convention No. 87, 26 January 2009.

[17] CEACR, Individual Observation concerning Freedom of Association and Protection of the Right to Organize Convention, 1948 No. 87 UK (ratification: 1949) Submitted: 2010, Document No. (ILOLEX): 062010GBR087. BALPA was quoted with preoccupations by the International Trade Union Confederation (ITUC): ITUC, *Internationally Recognised Core Labour Standards in the European Union: Report for the WTO General Council Review*, Geneva, 6–8 July 2011.

[18] A confirmation of this prediction is the long dispute between Lufthansa and the pilots union Cockpit, in which the discussion was on whether to consider legal the strike called to support the extension to a foreign subsidiary of the agreement signed for pilots employed by the mother company. A. Bücker, M. Hauer, and T. Walter, 'Workers' rights

Becoming the bearer of a new global wisdom, CEACR made its voice heard from Geneva, indirectly claiming to be in a privileged position to evaluate linkages and connections in global law. The experts went as far as advising that prevention of conflict should be preferred, for example identifying minimum services to be provided even in the course of industrial action.

The dispute went on because CEACR's reiterated recommendations to amend British law were disregarded. The Committee had, in fact, pointed to the inadequacy of the answers provided by the British government with regard to the deterrent impact of the announced injunctions and to the actions for damages threatened by the employer on the ground of *Viking* and *Laval*.[19] The experts were not satisfied with the subtle arguments put forward by the British government with regard to the proportionality test that was applied, in conformity with the CJEU's case law and in compliance of EU law. Obligations originated from membership of the EU were not compatible, in the government's view, with amendments to British legislation required by the experts in Geneva. There is a touch of hypocrisy in this approach, which recalls instrumentally the primacy of EU law, in order to keep the dispute within national borders, not listening to the voice of an authoritative international organisation.

Conflict 'in the skies' matches the metaphorical image of 'conflict in the seas' proposed in the previous chapter. Such metaphors are meant to recall that mobility in all its facets – and in the cases recalled in transport – stands as a key factor in modern conflicts and shapes the attitudes and the strategies of unions.

In 2009 the Finnish labour Court ruled in a case brought by the union of flight attendants. Finnair, the national airline, concluded an agreement with the Spanish company Air Europe, which also provided, as part of the services for the use of the airplanes, for the posting of cabin crew. The employees of Air Europe would have been covered by Spanish collective agreements, thus clashing with the Finnish collective agreement signed by Finnair. The latter provided the extension to posted workers of working conditions applicable in Finland.[20]

and economic freedoms: symphony or cacophony? A critical analysis from a German perspective', in A. Bücker and W. Warneck (eds.), *Reconciling Fundamental Social Rights and Economic Freedoms after Viking Laval Rüffert* (Baden Baden: Nomos 2011), 46 ff.

19 CEACR, Individual observation, supra n. 17.

20 See N. Bruun and C. M. Jonsson, 'Country Report: Nordic Countries', in Bücker and Warneck (eds.), *Viking, Laval, Rüffert*, supra n. 15, 24. Regulation (EU) No. 465/2012 of the European Parliament and of the Council of 22 May, on the coordination of social

The Court maintained that, to avoid a contrast with Article 56 TFEU, the Directive on the posting of workers should be interpreted on the basis of the CJEU's case law, thus corroborating Finnair's choice not to apply the Finnish collective agreement. This is yet another sign of the widespread implications of *Viking* and *Laval*, well beyond the original disputes which initiated the CJEU's rulings.

Back in Geneva, another impetuous voice was heard in the ILO.

During the 101st International Labour Conference,[21] employers' organisations, represented in the tripartite structure of the Conference and charged to examine the annual Report of the CEACR, harshly attacked the experts, challenging their extensive interpretation of the right to strike, whereas they should have restricted their monitoring to the application of ILO legal instruments. The attack went as far as refusing to discuss and adopt a list of twenty-five ILO member countries which had been accused of violating the Conventions.

This intervention was reported in the press as an anomalous one which had no precedent.[22] It proved to be a dis-function within the internal structure of the ILO, which should always respect the tripartite composition of this peculiar international organisation. The most startling aspect of this episode was that employers' organisations aimed, with a demonstrative gesture of unusual evidence, to take away from the experts their typical function, which consists in interpreting ILO sources, at an independent level, employing their legal expertise.

At the origin of this strong opposition carried on by the employers' group we find some of the issues dealt with before. Such organisations seem unprepared to take on board the progressive expansion of labour standards, through a circular and, at times, controversial contamination of sources. Pluralism is the key for understanding changes and capturing a dialectic which is going on among governments, the EU and international institutions, and courts at a national and supranational level.

The employers' group's not very convincing request was to impose on the experts a previous consultation of employers' and labour organisations, before entering their institutional task of monitoring the application of Conventions and Recommendations. This would have meant

security systems, introduced the criterion of the place where the service is provided, in order to determine the law applicable for cabin crews in civil aviation.

[21] International Labour Conference, Provisional Records, 101st Session, Geneva, May–June 2012.

[22] 'Les Travaux de l'OIT bloqués par des divergences sur le "droit de grève"', *Le Monde*, 18 June 2012.

imposing on an independent body, supportive of the Governing Board of the ILO, interpretative criteria not corroborated by legal expertise, but by partisan views. The exercise of this unprecedented vetoing power had the consequence of stopping the work of the CEACR and disseminated distrust and scepticism towards an authoritative international organisation.

This attack on tripartitism can be read as a reaction to the stronger evidence given to ILO standards in the ECtHR's rulings on the right to strike.[23] The unpredictability of this uncommon protest reopened the discussion on appeal to the International Court of Justice (ICJ) that ILO members can promote on questions of interpretation, an option not easy to follow and not favoured in the history of the ILO.[24]

The employers' group made a counterintuitive choice, compared to the trend chosen by large multinational companies, entering transnational collective agreements, which adopt as a point of reference fundamental rights recognised in ILO sources, as well as in the guidelines of the UN Global Compact and of the Ruggie Report.[25] On a different and not less significant ground, ILO standards had a wide circulation in EU countries badly affected by austerity measures during the economic and financial crisis. They counterbalanced too restrictive legal measures which were imposed by the European institutions.[26]

3 Voices and Threats: An Unbalanced Conflict

There are good reasons, as anticipated earlier on, to look with great attention into techniques enhancing a transnational consensus through new formulas, despite all complexities at stake. This proposition does not imply a thorough marginalisation of conflict. It moves into the direction of understanding the reasons behind new functions of industrial actions. Conflict is unbalanced when it enters the scene of the economic crisis and tries to fulfil emancipation of the weakest. Conflict is suspended between the fulfilment of their aspirations and limits put to it by financial constraints.

[23] C. La Hovary, 'Showdown at the ILO? A historical perspective on the employers' group's 2012 challenge to the right to strike', *Industrial Law Journal*, 42 (2013), 341–2.

[24] C. Hofmann, '(The right to) strike and the International Labour Organization' (F. Ebert Stiftung May 2014), library.fes.de/pdf-files/iez/10775.pdf.

[25] See Chapter 3, Section 2.1.

[26] A. Fisher Lescano, *Human Rights in Times of Austerity Policy. The EU Institutions and the Conclusion of Memoranda of Understanding* (Baden-Baden: Nomos 2014).

The hybridisation of supranational legal instruments supports a variety of argumentative methods because each of the normative systems taken into consideration is grounded on different premises and refers to the recipients of courts' decisions with functionally different messages.

This does not prevent convergence of international standards. For instance, freedom of association travelled from the Supreme Court of Canada,[27] to the Strasbourg Court and then to the ILO Committee of Experts. Later on the Italian Constitutional Court dealt with freedom of association and the right to bargain collectively in the public sector, following a long 'freeze' of negotiations as a consequence of financial restrictions.[28]

The Canadian Court modified its case law, which had been developing for over twenty years, whereby collective bargaining did not enter the area covered by freedom of association. It did so as a reaction to an insistent strategy of the unions, active to signal to the ILO the lack of respect of trade union rights by the federal and regional government. The Court, referring to Article 2 letter d of the Canadian Charter of Rights and Freedoms, declared that collective bargaining must be protected in its procedural function, regardless of its final objectives. Freedom of association is interpreted by the Court in its dynamic meaning, rather than focusing on collective agreements and on their economic impact. The acknowledgement of the duty to bargain in good faith allows only a 'limited' right, which is not wide enough to include the right to strike. In 2015 the Supreme Court of Canada expanded its previous interpretation, deciding a case on the right to strike in essential services. A majority of judges considered that the right to strike is not 'merely derivative of collective bargaining', but constitutes an 'indispensable component

[27] Supreme Court of Canada, *Health Services and Support – Facilities Subsector Bargaining Association* v. *British Columbia* (2007), 2 SCR, 291 27, commented by J. Fudge, 'The Supreme Court of Canada and the right to bargain collectively: the implications of the Health Services and Support case in Canada and beyond', *Industrial Law Journal*, 37 (2008), 25. In Canada there is a vivacious discussion on the constitutionalisation of social rights after the entry into force in 1982 of the Charter of Rights and Freedoms. See: J. Fudge, 'Constitutionalizing labour rights in Europe', in T. Campbell, K. D. Ewing, and A. Tomkins (eds.), *The Legal Protection of Human Rights: Sceptical Essays* (Oxford University Press 2011). In *Fraser* v. *Ontario* 2011, 2 SCR, 3, the Court insinuated some doubts on its previous case law. See: A. Bogg and K. Ewing, 'A (muted) voice at work? Collective bargaining in the Supreme Court of Canada', *Comparative Labor Law and Policy Journal*, 33 (2012), 379 ff.

[28] Corte Costituzionale, judgment 178/2015, www.cortecostituzionale.it/documenti/download/doc/recent_judgments/S178_2015_en.pdf. See Chapter 1.

of that right'. The test on whether there is an infringement of section 2(d) of the Charter consists in verifying whether there is a 'substantial interference' with collective bargaining.[29]

The Canadian examples suggest that recognising a duty to bargain and expanding the function of the right to strike in essential services are significant steps towards the identification of freedom of association as a grounding principle. However, recognising a duty to bargain is not an insignificant step towards the identification of freedom of association as a grounding principle. Trade unions, identified as negotiators and holders of the right to strike, can be exposed to contradictory interventions of the courts. This explains the aspiration to listen to ever-clearer messages from supranational courts, in order to develop a comprehensive definition of freedom of association.

In this picture of lights and shadows, a preliminary conclusion can be suggested. The resonance provoked by the method of balancing social rights and economic freedoms should not be amplified too much. Such a method, mirrored in a questionable way in the case law of the Luxembourg Court, is not irreversible. Accordingly, the fear that the grey shadow of a controversial case law could expand beyond EU borders should be put into a pragmatic perspective, looking to other paths opened in Strasbourg and Geneva.

EU internal market law finds its limits in the 'safety valve' of justification, related – among other criteria – to respect for national institutions and for the delicate balance they establish whenever transnational issues are at stake. This approach, which is typically echoed in the CJEU's case law, was not followed in *Viking* and *Laval*.[30]

Hence, a wave of fear hit the organisations representing workers all over Europe and prompted an institutional reaction through the Monti Report. Political institutions were not able to answer rapidly to the suggestions put forward in that authoritative policy document. Proposals to modify the Directive on posting of workers were slowly put through the decision-making machinery.[31] The regulation on the

[29] *Saskatchewan Federation of Labour* v. *Saskatchewan*, 2015 SCC 4, [2015] 1 SCR 245.

[30] S. Weatherill, 'The EU Internal Market Perspective', in M. Freedland and J. Prassl (eds.), *Viking, Laval and Beyond* (Oxford: Hart Publishing 2015), 34–6.

[31] Directive 2014/67 /EU of the European Parliament and of the Council of 15 May 2014 on the enforcement of Directive 96/71/EC concerning the posting of workers in the framework of the provision of services and amending Regulation (EU) No. 1024/2012 on administrative cooperation through the Internal Market Information System ('the IMI Regulation') currently undergoing further revisions.

exercise of the right to strike in the context of the freedom of establishment and freedom to provide services had to undergo equally difficult tests.[32]

On the basis of previous proposals, inspired by Monti, at the time acting as a European Commissioner and aiming to make the right to strike compatible with the free movement of goods,[33] the Commission set an analogous objective in the so-called Monti II Regulation. The idea was, once more, to enhance the construction of a social market economy and guarantee that in exercising the right to strike, the principle of proportionality should be respected and so should national laws and constitutional values.

However, all good intentions to correct the wrong impact of the Court's case law, putting forward new solutions based on conciliatory measures, were nullified by strong political opposition shown by national parliaments. The Commission was forced to withdraw the proposal, taking on board criticism on issues, such as the choice of the legal basis and EU competence to legislate.[34]

Proposals to revise the Directive on the posting of workers, following the 2014 Enforcement Directive,[35] had to overcome an equally strong opposition, caused by cautious national reactions mainly related to the enforcement of the equal treatment principle in host countries. The Commission's proposals were supported by research, which confirmed the centrality of all issues at stake in national discussions and represented a valid background to on-going negotiations. The reform of posting of workers presented by the Commission,[36] accompanied by an impact assessment,[37] has become a ground for critical reflection at national

[32] European Commission, Proposal for a Council Regulation on the exercise of the right to take collective action within the context of the freedom of establishment and the freedom to provide services, *COM* (2012) 130 final, 21 March 2012. For a critical overview see K. Ewing, *The Draft Monti II Regulation: An Inadequate Response to Viking and Laval* (Liverpool: Institute of Employment Rights 2011).

[33] Regulation (EC) No. 2679/98 of the Council of 7 December 1998 on the functioning of the internal market in relation to the free movement of goods among the Member States.

[34] Withdrawal COM (2012) 130, 2012/0061/COD OJ C 109, 16 April 2013.

[35] Directive 2014/67/EU of the European Parliament and of the Council of 15 May 2014 on the enforcement of Directive 96/71/EC concerning the posting of workers in the framework of the provision of services and amending Regulation (EU) No. 1024/2012 on administrative cooperation through the Internal Market Information System ('the IMI Regulation').

[36] Proposal for a Directive of the European Parliament and of the Council amending Directive 96/71/EC, COM (2016) 128 final, of 8 March 2016.

[37] European Commission, *Impact Assessment accompanying the document Proposal for a Directive of the European Parliament and the Council amending Directive 96/71/EC*

level and has now generated the necessary consensus towards the formal adoption of a new Directive.

4 Pre-occupied Voices and Limits to Conflict

It is difficult to deny that the case law of the Luxembourg court, which was explored in the previous pages, represents, even after several years, an obstacle for a full consolidation of fundamental social rights. Europe, speaking with the voice of its supranational judges, used tones not always tuned into national identities and constitutional traditions.

It is certainly relevant that the Charter of Fundamental Rights, which has now acquired the same legal value of primary EU law, should be perceived as an integral part of global law. References to it made by the Strasbourg Court in *Demir* are promising. The Charter is constantly enriched along the years through a consistent case law, which should be assessed as a necessary follow-up.[38]

The central issue, on which commentators are concentrating, concerns the full inclusion of the right to strike within a supranational body of norms regulating labour in its individual and collective implications. The interpreters of global law do not prefer a formalistic definition of the right to strike, grounded on previous traditions of countervailing powers, but rather to its being actionable when a transnational dimension of the interests to be protected is at stake.

Voices from the two European courts were listened to with caution. The contradictory messages delivered by them show, in fact, a slow transformation of a model. New ways of exercising industrial action, if interpreted proportionally in order not to collide with economic freedoms within the EU internal market, can hide destabilising effects on national systems of industrial relations. Fears, primarily referring to the loss of centrality of the right to strike, are mirrored in the parallel right to collective bargaining. The two dimensions of rights exercised collectively are included, and not by chance, with different nuances in the reasoning developed by the CJEU.

The idea that a crucial function of the right to strike, seen as a unique and powerful sanction against the employers, should be lost, seems a point of no return or, to use a recurring metaphor, a tunnel without an exit.

concerning the posting of workers in the framework of the provision of services SWD (2016) 53 final.

[38] See fra.europa.eu/en/case-law-database.

For many generations of labour lawyers in Western Europe conflict represented a cornerstone, since it stabilised and strengthened systems of collective bargaining. From the emancipatory social function of conflict, the narrative of labour law developed into a pluralist and open vision of society in the years following the end of the Second World War. The equilibrium of powers in collective bargaining reflects a wider notion of democracy, inclusive and attentive to the aspirations of individuals and of representative organisations.

A recurring preoccupation is, and not by chance, fomented by judges, capable of preoccupying the social and factual territory on which, without external intrusions, conflict should express itself freely. This is why, in the opinion of some scholars, the innovative case law of the Strasbourg Court on freedom of association could become a new argumentative trap which does not allow an evolving interpretation, but simply envisages future judicial drifts. There would be, in other words, a reticence in accepting the message of supranational courts by national judges, the latter being too concentrated on solving domestic disputes.[39]

However, Article 11 of the ECHR, and its interpretation provided by the Strasbourg Court, has been gradually receiving wider recognition.[40] From an 'individualistic' interpretation based on the protection of the negative freedom of association, there has been a move towards a collective dimension, which includes the right to strike. Both interpretations reflect the double function of freedom of association, which is addressed, both to individuals, entitled with positive and negative freedoms, and to organisations, entitled with a collective right.

The two sides of freedom of association were expanded by the Strasbourg Court in different historical times, with the objective of indicating an evolution, which also acknowledges in recent decisions a stronger interconnection between national and supranational norms.

A different preoccupation is at the origin of criticism expressed towards the case law of the Luxembourg Court. It has to do with its deterrent and even intimidating effect, with respect to national unions, which feel inhibited in exercising the right to strike and consequently

39 Ewing and Hendy, 'The dramatic implications', supra n. 12. Further references to the United Kingdom in L. Hayes, T. Novitz, and H. Reed, 'Applying the Laval quartet in a UK context: chilling, ripple and disruptive effects in industrial relations', in Bücker and Warneck (eds.), *Reconciling Fundamental Social Rights*, supra n. 18, 220.

40 F. Dorssemont, K. Lörcher, and I. Schömann (eds.), *The European Convention on Human Rights and the Employment Relation* (Oxford: Hart Publishing 2013).

deprived of a crucial function. In other words, the Luxembourg Court, inducing trade unions to desist from industrial action, introduced a subtle threat, which could, in the long term, weaken the role of the unions.

Even more preoccupying are the unknown cases, the ones that do not appear in courts as a consequence of the threats sent from Luxembourg, ending in the loss of visibility of the unions.[41]

In this context of pervading tensions, the unusual position taken by the employers' group at the ILO represents yet another disruptive element. That signal is profoundly damaging to the role of a tripartite organisation such as the ILO, due to perform its function as a *super partes* institution.

In the difficult evolution of European social policies, with the intent to reconcile the many different directions taken by the same, it is urgent to go beyond preoccupied disputes and pay attention to the evolution of the right to strike. One possible reaction of national legal systems to the CJEU's controversial case law can be to look at ways to introduce obligatory conciliation or mediation and to enhance measures supportive of collective bargaining.[42]

A pragmatic approach to the evolution of conflict takes into account all new constraints imposed on national systems of industrial relations. National and transnational regimes of solidarity have been disconnected. The economic and financial crisis has reshaped traditional definitions of conflict, while accentuating a harsh confrontation among different groups of workers, some of which find themselves in a more marginalised position than others within labour markets.

The aim towards emancipation, that conflict typically pursues, is still impellent as it is the quest for a more equitable social justice. However, the right to strike could reveal itself as inadequate in interpreting the expectations of workers, in cases, such as the ones described in *Viking*

[41] A comparative analysis, on potential implications of *Viking* and *Laval* is in B. Adell, F. Hendricks, and S. L. Willborn, 'Three perspectives on the Viking and Laval decisions', *Comparative Labor Law and Policy Journal*, 32 (2011), 1023 ff. Aware of the complexities inherent in a comparison with federal systems, the authors nevertheless reflect upon the hypothetical impact of *Viking* and *Laval* on Canada and the United States.

[42] B. Hepple, 'Rethinking laws against strikes', in A. Kerr (ed.), *The Industrial Relations Act 1990: 20 Years On* (Dublin: Round Hall and Thomson Reuters 2010); L. Corazza, 'In search of industrial self-regulation or efficient settlement of employment disputes? The case of Italian arbitration reform', *Comparative Labor Law and Policy Journal*, 33 (2012), 245 ff. In *BALPA* the ILO Committee of Experts went as far as suggesting that limits should be set to the right to strike.

and *Laval*, in which collective interests cross national borders. There is not a transnational dimension of conflict, but the interpretation of international standards is becoming more inclusive. Conflict is the essence of many contradictions, originated by the crisis and by attempts to impose a race to the bottom in competing regimes of solidarity.

6

Integration and Disintegration

Concluding Remarks

1 Keywords: Solidarity and Conflict

In previous chapters existing social and employment policies have been tackled, with the intention to show potential synergies among them and ascertain how to fulfil a coherent project. The main purpose behind such a reconsideration of recent choices made at EU level is to prove that there has been a constant move towards reforms and innovations. These efforts have, nevertheless, hit the hard reality of slow enforcement mechanisms and of uneven communication between the centre and the periphery of the Union. The declining project for a closer political Union has been accompanied by the harsh consequences of the crisis and by the impact of austerity measures on countries undergoing financial difficulties. Disillusion was spread among European citizens and fears were accentuated by the lack of a vision for the future. The crisis heightened differences among national economies and increased the divides within the population.

Solidarity and conflict are the keywords chosen to highlight all contradictions emerging in European social and employment policies in the aftermath of the crisis. They are also chosen to fight back disintegration within the EU and accomplish new ways ahead for integration.

Solidarity has been taken as the key to detect the emergence of collective interests, either through existing systems of collective bargaining at national level, or through European sector agreements or even through new forms of transnational agreements. Threats to solidarity have come from wage competition and more broadly from social dumping.

These signs of disintegration should be contrasted, at least in part, by the reform of the posting of workers Directive. Consensus has now been reached on the necessary amendments, precisely on the controversial issues of remuneration and the length of posting in the receiving country. In the last few years, national solutions to contrast social dumping have been proposed in some Scandinavian countries.[1] They

[1] See Chapter 4.

mainly rely on collective agreements or on state agencies that should introduce equitable clarifications for low-paid workers posted from other EU countries. The Council of Nordic Trade Unions is a good example of synergies on EU policies. This collaboration should be enhanced in furthering already existing contacts with neighbouring trade unions, such as the Baltic Sea Trade Union Network. Social dialogue must continue to be a valuable option in building consensus and promoting encompassing wage policies.

Conflict – and in particular the right to strike – has been at the core of the CJEU's judgments, which have proposed a balance against market freedoms. This case law had important consequences for its deterrent effect on national unions and for the reaction of the employers' group within the ILO. Conflict here opens national scenarios, in which the right to strike is embedded in constitutional traditions and relies on high union membership. An issue of credibility of the unions towards their members is crucial and so is their bargaining power, which is preserved as an essential asset.

The chain of events generated by the CJEU's rulings is unique and has been described in some detail with the intention to document inter-institutional and inter-courts reactions. Critics of the Court's attitude in *Viking, Laval* and in other later cases have insinuated reservations well beyond the impact of the rulings, assuming irreversible threats to national systems of fundamental rights and a progressive marginalisation of conflict. Hence, the paradigm of solidarity, a founding value of the EU, supported by industrial action, an exceptional resource to enforce such a value, has been covered by a shade of disillusion.

The analysis suggested in this book is that the Court's rulings have preceded even more disruptive events occurring during the economic and financial crisis. In countries severely hit by the crisis social unrest was widespread and often took the form of spontaneous protests. The awareness of insecurity among weak and marginal groups of citizens has been perceptible and has caused some reconsideration of the policies to be adopted. 'The Five Presidents' Report on Completing Europe's EMU', delivered in June 2015[2] is a relevant document in setting the new scene and involving in this critical effort all EU institutions.

Self-analysis at EU level was also triggered by national constitutional courts and, in a different way, by international organisations asked to

[2] *The Five Presidents' Report: Completing Europe's Economic and Monetary Union*, ec.europa.eu/commission/publications/five-presidents-report-completing-europes-economic-and-monetary-union_en.

intervene in the evaluation of violations inflicted on labour standards and fundamental social rights.

2 Constitutional Adjudication in the Crisis

The equilibrium of opposite, potentially contraposed powers in collective bargaining is the emblem of a wider notion of democracy, inclusive and attentive to the aspirations of individuals and of representative organisations. This has been one of the goals achieved in European countries fighting against dictatorship, in which, after the Second World War, constitutions inclusive of social rights were adopted.[3] It is also for this historical reason that constitutional courts have acted responsibly in Western European democracies and have established their own legitimacy, ensuring transparency in their own decision-making techniques and strengthening their reputations, based on competence and independence.[4] There is no lack of accountability in the trajectories of constitutional adjudication that each court has created, in accordance with national traditions.

Consequences brought about by the crisis in countries undergoing severe economic difficulties gave new visibility to constitutional adjudication, in ways that may have accentuated their participation in law-making. Whereas parliaments were put under pressure to comply with strict deadlines for the adoption of austerity measures, constitutional courts were asked to review imbalances and to bring back equilibrium within national legal systems, whenever infringements of constitutional rights had occurred.[5] This, too, is a fully accountable process, which preserves the rule of law and strengthens parliamentary discretionary powers.[6]

[3] O. Kahn-Freund, 'The impact of constitutions on labour law', *Cambridge Law Journal*, 35 (1976), 240 ff; B. Hepple, *Labour Laws and Global Trade* (Oxford: Hart Publishing 2005).

[4] A summary of a comparative analysis oriented into this direction is in P. Pasquino, 'A political theory of constitutional democracy: on legitimacy of constitutional courts in stable liberal democracies', in T. Christiano, I. Creppell, and J. Knight (eds.), *Morality Governance, and Social Institutions* (Basingstoke: Palgrave Macmillan 2018), 197–232.

[5] 'Constitutional integrity' inspired adjudication in all such cases, as reported by C. Kilpatrick, 'Constitutions, social rights and sovereign debt crisis in Europe: a challenging new area of constitutional inquiry', EUI Working Papers, Law 34/2015.

[6] A sign of closer cooperation has been offered by constitutional courts, lodging preliminary references to the CJEU. Some examples in S. Sciarra and G. Nicastro, '"Speech acts" and judicial conversations. Preliminary references from the Italian Constitutional Court to the Court of Justice of the European Union', www.csfederalismo.it/it/pubblicazioni/csf-sssp-wp-series/1127-speech-acts-and-judicial-conversations-preliminary-references-from-the-italian-constitutional-court-to-the-court-of-justice-of-the-european-union.

The dilemma faced by individual workers and by large organisations representing them during the crisis, notwithstanding national constitutions, has often coincided with disaffection for Europe. Europe generated fears among citizens. Particularly those who were envisaging social justice and emancipation as an encompassing design pursued by European institutions, became sceptical about further projects of integration.

Solidarity regimes were shaken and broken up in contradictory ways. Inequalities emerged as a consequence of social dumping and wage competition. Fundamental rights were seriously endangered because of austerity measures. Such measures were often addressed towards the middle class, hitting pensioners and public sector workers. They also affected resources to fight poverty and to give access to essential social services.

Contradictions underpinning such political choices are many. In the attempt to select the cohorts of citizens towards which sacrifices should be addressed, for example the public sector workers allegedly more secure in their positions than others, legislators could not ignore respect for the principle of equality, which stays at the core of European constitutionalism, as does the principle of proportionality.

The proportionality test faced by constitutional courts conforms to the intensity of reductions or even permanent cuts in public spending. It is often accompanied by the evaluation of the urgency required to fulfil obligations originated by membership of the EU. Time required for the enforcement of austerity measures must be balanced against the infringements of rights and expectations. Reductions in pensions and pay freezes in the public sector, if enforced for a limited time, have been held constitutional.

Time can also become relevant in deciding the postponed enforceability of constitutional rulings. This particular technique can raise problems for a potentially too wide discretion acquired by constitutional courts in derogating from traditional criteria. It is justified though by budgetary restrictions, which courts often take into account in order not to disrupt the symmetry of powers exercised by parliaments.

At this regard, the newly constituted network of fiscal councils could become, if properly empowered by states, a *super partes* reference point. Competence and independence from political affiliations should be the resources to rely on, whenever objective data must be produced and made available for institutional purposes. Constitutional courts are cautious in letting economic and financial reasons prevail on the adjudication of constitutional rights. Hence, balancing is a necessary exercise and has specific peculiarities in each case considered by the courts. Objective information and reliable data are, therefore, relevant when kept in the background of Constitutional courts' judgments, in particular when a proportionality test is applied in cases of sharp imbalances between the cost of economic manoeuvres and their impact on constitutional rights.

Precisely because of all such inherent contradictions in the strategies put in place by legislators, national constitutional courts have been called to play a central role[7] and so have international organisations enforcing labour standards. Judicial and quasi-judicial activism has reinvigorated the circulation of international standards and provoked a beneficial contamination of legal sources.

However, a most surprising discovery emerging from this interplay of legal sources is the uncertainty that often surrounds the scope and enforceability of EU law.

A Report prepared for the Petition Committee of the European Parliament shows the uneasiness of EU institutions in answering back to specific requests. For example, no answers were given to Greek petitioners, who saw the right to collective bargaining, guaranteed in Article 28 of the EU Charter of Fundamental Rights, dangerously jeopardised by austerity measures.[8] In this case – the Commission replied – national measures taken in compliance of a MoU signed by Greece within the scheme of the EFSF, fell outside the implementation of EU law for the purpose of Article 51 of the Charter of Fundamental Rights.

All such uncertainties are behind the EP's request to start an inter-institutional discussion on the establishment of an EU mechanism on democracy, the rule of law and fundamental rights[9] and it is noteworthy that this request follows a previous opinion delivered by the Economic and Social Committee.[10] The CJEU's ruling in *Florescu* offers convincing arguments in favour of the inclusion of austerity measures – adopted in compliance of the obligations subscribed to in MoUs outside the Eurozone – within EU law and consequently within the Court's competence.[11]

[7] C. Fasone, *Constitutional Courts Facing the Euro Crisis. Italy, Portugal and Spain in a Comparative Perspective*. EUI Working Papers 15/2014.

[8] E. Spaventa, *The interpretation of Article 51 of the EU Charter of Fundamental Rights: the dilemma of stricter or broader application of the Charter to national measures. A study promoted by the Petition Committee of the European Parliament*, February 2016.

[9] See www.europarl.europa.eu/oeil/popups/ficheprocedure.do?reference=2015/2254(INL)&l=en#documentGateway.

[10] SOC/536 European control mechanism on the rule of law and fundamental rights, adopted on 19 October 2016.

[11] See Chapter 1, Section 2.3.

The margin of appreciation that the CJEU recognises to national legislators is a security valve and fortifies the balance of powers between parliaments and the judiciary. In *Florescu* the Court explicitly stated its own intention not to interfere with the priorities set by the national legislator in deciding how to reduce the balance of payments, which was at the origin of requests of financial assistance to Romania. The law in question – the Court indicates – was temporary and had an exceptional nature, as it frequently happens with the planning of austerity measures by national governments. Relinquishing a parallel income for a paid professional activity with a public institution was the alternative required if the pensioners in question sought to continue receiving a full pension.

On similar lines, the Italian Constitutional Court held constitutional legislation – first entered into force in 2011 and reiterated in 2014 – which set an upper threshold on remunerations within the public sector and a maximum limit for the cumulative total of remuneration and pensions. The test, in this case, was on reasonableness of the measures adopted, all aimed at the rationalisation of public spending, under restricted resources.[12]

Neither an analogy, nor a comparative evaluation of the two cases, should be suggested. Each court, be it national or supranational, is grounded on different premises and carries specific competences, which also imply the adoption of different arguments and techniques of adjudication. For these reasons, it is informative to enrich the inventory of such techniques and to expand the research on arguments offered by judges, when they are faced with the pressures of measures adopted in exceptional circumstances. Judicial strategies have, by all means, been relevant to re-establish a balance and to broaden the interpretation of EU law during the crisis.

3 European Deliberative Processes Re-politicised: The European Pillar of Social Rights

All different existing EU policies scrutinised in this book offer an opportunity to reclaim national democratic traditions and feed again a positive and constructive discourse on European integration. A few points emerge from such scrutiny and can be briefly summarised.

[12] Italian Constitutional Court, Judgment 124/2017; English translation at: www.cortecostituzionale.it/documenti/download/doc/recent_judgments/S_124_2017_EN.pdf.

First of all, a critical appraisal of European developments reveals that the construction of a monetary union should have been accompanied by an integrated Europe of fiscal policies and that more should have been done in boosting social policies. A prevailing reaction to the crisis was the enforcement of intergovernmental projects, distant from a typical European method. This choice is problematic in the long run, particularly if one considers the risk of marginalising the EP and delegitimising European institutions.

I have insisted on a subtle and yet persistent de-politicisation of European policies, with a special attention to events that have decoupled social and employment matters from political deliberations. Notwithstanding this criticism, I have also attempted to indicate how fears coming from Europe and spreading among citizens should be progressively abandoned and addressed towards more promising visions of the future.

With special reference to employment policies, I have argued that a new emphasis on hard law should not be seen as a total defeat of governance deliberative techniques. The opening up to civil society and to processes of mutual learning, proposed as a turning point at the beginning of the year 2000, contributed to de-politicising deliberations within the EU institutions and weakened real efforts of coordination among national administrations. The attempt to enhance mixed administration within the EU and methodically include national apparatuses within supranational decision-making was not successful in the enforcement of employment policies.

The OMC was expanded to other fields of European policies and was pictured for many years as the proper answer to a deficient agenda of social law, when unemployment was rising and discontent was diffused among citizens. The attractiveness of OMC was in its premises, which consisted in the effort to expand criteria of representation of collective interests and open up the system to civil society. In this expanded practice of deliberative democracy concrete and well-defined criteria of representativeness were, at times, under-evaluated and so was the outcome of processes of norm setting, in which decisions must be based on full legitimacy.

The OMC was overly emphasised by political scientists, who were critical of previous forms of interest representation within EU institutions. The frequent delegation of decisions to committees had, for many years, been the object of discussions in academic circles and among policy-makers. The perceived risk in such a diffused system of delegations, accompanying all stages of decision-making, was to deprive institutions of their political power, expanding technocratic approaches to EU policies.

The severe impact of the crisis requires reconsidering employment policies and the overall rationale supporting the OMC. The main elements that must characterise this reassessment are, on the one hand, an excessive reliance on the perfect mix of so-called flexicurity measures and, on the other, an insufficient and delayed planning on the promotion of new skills for new occupations. The revised version of the European qualification framework, adopted on 24 May 2017, shows renewed attention on this issue.[13]

To address the dramatic consequences of youth unemployment, worsened during the crisis, support for training was in part oriented towards school leavers and projected into the future with programmes of life-long learning. This perspective, which has repeatedly been included in European agendas, should continue to be a priority, particularly for shaping new ideas on the future of work in the 'sharing economy'.

Another point to underline in reassessing active labour market policies is the shift to hard law, which should also favour the exchange of reliable information among national administrations. In recent years the choice has been made to intervene on these matters adopting Decisions, binding on Member States in their entirety. This happened with the setting up of the network of public employment services and the parallel network of EURES, in view of further favouring interactions among public and private bodies.

An additional step in re-visiting active employment policies and strengthening integration can go as far as introducing a 'European Unemployment Benefit Scheme'.[14] Part of the 2012 Commission's proposal to reinforce the social dimension of EMU, the idea has now become even more timely. Support to euro area Member States undergoing fiscal constraints should be provided, in order to avoid cuts of automatic stabilisers and reduce negative spill overs in the crisis. The underpinning to such proposal, addressed at short-term cyclical unemployment only, is

[13] See Chapter 2.

[14] The proposal, first released by the Italian Minister of finance in October 2015, has been further developed: www.mef.gov.it/inevidenza/documenti/Unemployment_benefit_scheme_rev_2016.pdf. It was also discussed in academic projects and in a working paper produced by the Centre for European Policy Studies, under the auspices of the European Commission: M. Beblavý, G. Marconi, and I. Maselli, *A European Unemployment Benefit Scheme. The Rationale and the Challenges Ahead* (Brussels August 2015).

the spreading of benefits to countries not in need of support, but interested in a stable macroeconomic environment. The impact of this measure on national labour markets is expected to be positive. It could promote more efficient reforms of labour markets and avoid the likelihood of structural unemployment, thus abandoning negative visions of disintegration.

Harmonisation through the adoption of Directives has been a more difficult objective to reach. This, too, could be perceived as a sign of disintegration, if we look, as we did in previous chapters, at the many difficulties encountered in the adoption of a revised Directive on posting of workers in a free provision of services. The initiative of social partners in neighbouring countries and the promotion of collective bargaining to reach common standards can be imperative in addressing the comparability of labour standards and wages. But hard law is pivotal to stable solutions in this crucial area of European social policies and constitutes an indispensable instrument for positive integration.

In order to re-politicise deliberations in all the areas discussed so far and in many more, the adoption of a pragmatic view and of shared consensus is needed. The urgency to anticipate changes, rather than intervene with passive measures in support of marginal groups, inspires new reformist agendas in ways that should foster growth and increase productivity. The pursuit of egalitarian objectives rescuing the most disadvantaged groups from a condition of marginality and under-representation should be part of political decisions.

All anticipatory and preventive measures must be longsighted and look beyond individual nation-states. They should take into account workers' mobility and the development of transnational chains of production. To think in transnational terms, however, does not imply predicting 'the end of states'. Private organisations pursuing egalitarian policies and trade unions promoting wage setting through collective bargaining must derive their legitimacy from states. I have produced examples of transnational collective agreements and insisted on the need to provide a European legal framework for such new experiments in collective autonomy.

These new developments, which mainly follow the impulse of large multinationals, confirm the role of states as coordinators of private denationalised entities and are meant to contrast incomplete theories on governance. As with the policy recommendations of the UN Ruggie Report, the aim should be to combine voluntary and binding legal instruments in pursuing respect for fundamental rights.

Legitimacy in processes of norm setting is generated by states and is grounded in national constitutional traditions. Re-politicising EU decision-making implies an expansion of hard law in areas of social and employment policies and a link to incentives provided by structural funds, in particular by the European Social Fund.

In his State of the Union address on 9 September 2015, the President of the Commission Juncker announced the establishment of a 'European Pillar of Social Rights', initially limited to the euro area countries and then open to other Member States willing to join. The social partners were mentioned as key actors in promoting new convergences. The 2016 Annual Growth Survey followed this programme and declared the intention to promote structural reforms, with an accent on social matters. This was the necessary follow-up to 'The Five Presidents' Report on Completing Europe's EMU' delivered in June 2015.

The Commission's Communication,[15] which launched the consultation on this new agenda, explicitly states that policies of flexicurity need to be reconsidered in the aftermath of the crisis and points to 'job and income security' as a prevailing interest for workers, while confirming the option for more inclusive labour markets, development of skills and social cohesion. Optimism pervades this document, which seems to imply that the page of the economic and financial crisis could be turned. However, as I have underlined in describing previous experiments in policy-making, facts do not always follow promises.

Credibility for such renewed promises should come from the commitment shown by the same Commission in making structural and investment funds available for social policies in the 2014–2020 budget. Furthermore, the new impetus consists in complementing the EU level existing social 'acquis', a straightforward proposal, which is not meant to dismantle existing policies. The following Commission's Recommendation, built around twenty principles, should inspire future actions and initiatives, both at EU and Member States level.[16] This new sign of a shared commitment goes into the direction of closer coordination and better integration. It also acknowledges the indispensable contribution of other international organisations. It is also noteworthy that, in delivering his 2017 'State of the

[15] Communication from the Commission to the European Parliament, the Council, the European Economic and Social Committee and the Committee of the Regions, Launching a consultation on a European Pillar of Social Rights, COM (2016) 127 final, Strasbourg 8 March 2016.

[16] Commission Recommendation of 26 April 2017 on the European Pillar of Social Rights, COM (2017) 2600 final.

Union' speech, the President of the Commission affirmed that 'in a Union of equals, there can be no second class workers' and explicitly referred to equality in wages, especially when mobility of workers is at stake. Hence, the proposal is to introduce a 'common labour authority' for fairer rules in the internal market.[17]

If this new announcement could be promptly implemented, some of the issues discussed in this book could be placed in a different context.

These are all good reasons to look ahead and set aside fears and disillusion.

[17] J.-C. Juncker, 'State of the Union Address', 13 September 2017, europa.eu/rapid/press-release_SPEECH-17-3165_en.htm. At the Employment, Social Policy, Health and Consumer Affairs Council of 23 October 2017, EU Ministers of Employment and Social Affairs expressed unanimous endorsement of the European Pillar of Social Rights and reached an agreement on the amendments to the Posted Workers Directive.

INDEX

Lightning Source UK Ltd.
Milton Keynes UK
UKHW020125121120
373246UK00009B/137

9 781107 450530